De Benneville R. Keim

A Guide to the Potomac River

Chesapeake bay and James river, and an ocean voyage to northern ports.

A series of interesting and instructive excursions by water from

Washington

De Benneville R. Keim

A Guide to the Potomac River
Chesapeake bay and James river, and an ocean voyage to northern ports. A series of interesting and instructive excursions by water from Washington

ISBN/EAN: 9783337302436

Printed in Europe, USA, Canada, Australia, Japan

Cover: Foto ©Andreas Hilbeck / pixelio.de

More available books at **www.hansebooks.com**

THE

POTOMAC RIVER,

CHESAPEAKE BAY AND JAMES RIVER,

AND

AN OCEAN VOYAGE

TO

NORTHERN PORTS.

A SERIES OF INTERESTING AND INSTRUCTIVE EXCURSIONS
BY WATER FROM WASHINGTON.

BY DE B. RANDOLPH KEIM.

(Washington Correspondent.)
Compiler of " Keim's Hand-Book of Washington and Its Environs,"
" Washington Illustrated," etc., etc.

WASHINGTON, D. C.:
BY THE COMPILER.

BALTIMORE

WASHINGTON
Georgetown
ALEXANDRIA
Mt. Vernon

ANNAPOLIS

EASTON

Herring Bay
Holland's Pt.
Poplar I.
Tilghman

Cook's Pt.

Cambridge

FREDERICKSBURG
Port Royal

Cove Pt.

Cedar Pt.

Pt. No Point

Pt. Lookout

Tappahannock

Smith's Pt.

Tangier I.

Watts' I.

RICHMOND
West Pt.

PETERSBURG
Yorktown

Hampton Roads

NORFOLK
Portsmouth

STATUTE MILES

CONTENTS.

PAGE.

AN HISTORICAL PREFACE 5

Engraving.—The Potomac in front of Washington, 4.

INTRODUCTORY INFORMATION 7

THE POTOMAC RIVER 9

Engravings.—The Capitol, 9. The Executive Mansion, 11.

EXCURSION I. From Washington to the Great Falls
of the Potomac 13

Engravings.—Georgetown and Aqueduct, 13. Cabin John Bridge, 16.
The Great Falls of the Potomac, 17.

EXCURSION II. From Washington to the mouth of
the Potomac 19

Engravings.—Arlington, 20. Washington from the Potomac, 21. The
mouth of the Anacostia River. 21. The United States Barracks, 22.
The Navy Yard; 23. Alexandria, 25. Fort Foote, 26. Fort Washington, 27. Mount Vernon from the river, 28. Same from the Alexandria road, 29. Indian Head, 31. The Possum Nose, 33. Quantico,
5. Aquia Creek, 37. Matthias Point, 39. Nomini Cliffs, 41.
Washington's Birthplace—1881, 43. Same—1732, 45. Blackistone
Island, 47. Piney Point, 48. Priest's Point, 49.

EXCURSION III. From Washington to Fortress
Monroe and Norfolk. 51

Engravings.—Smith's Point, 53. Fortress Monroe, 55.

EXCURSION IV. From Washington to Richmond. . 61

Engravings.—Jamestown Island, 63. Ruins of Jamestown, 65. Har-
son's Landing, 67.

EXCURSION V. From Washington to Philadelphia,
New York, and Boston by sea.. . . . . . , 71

Engravings.—Cape Charles, 72. Cape Henry, 73.

EXCURSION VI. From Washington to Baltimore. 75

Engravings—Mouth of the Patuxent, 76. Mouth of the Severn, 77. Highlands of the Magothy, 78. Entrance to the Patapsco, 79. Baltimore from
the Harbor, 79.

(3)

THE POTOMAC RIVER IN FRONT OF WASHINGTON.

An Historical Preface.

THE annually increasing interest of the traveling public in the POTOMAC RIVER and CHESAPEAKE BAY, and the demand for a reliable HAND-BOOK of *popular information* on these water routes leading from the governing city of the Nation to the ocean, has suggested to the compiler the preparation of this little work as a companion to his comprehensive Hand-book of Washington and its environs.

The entire surface of this mundane sphere presents no expanse of inland water more beautiful to the eye, more munificently endowed with aquatic wealth, and, at the same time, more replete with tradition and history, than the great Bay of Chesapeake, and those magnificent fluvial highways, the Potomac and the James, tributary to it. Upon the banks of the James the first germ of English colonization took root upon the virgin soil of the New World. It is true that Menendez, under the auspices of Spain, had established the first settlement from the Old World at St. Augustine, in sunny Florida, in 1565; that Espejo, from among the Spanish conquerors of Mexico, had founded Santa Fè, in the very heart of the continent, in 1583, and that Port Royal, in Nova Scotia, in 1605, was made a permanent settlement under the royal standard of France; but Jamestown, on the James river, in Virginia, was the first permanent settlement of that race in whose veins coursed the rich admixture of Anglo-Saxon blood—a people foremost in colonization, foremost in the civilization of the age, and ultimately, by prowess of intellect and force, the dominant race on the fairest portions of the North American continent.

More than a decade before the Puritans of the Mayflower, under the civil and religious leadership of Carver and Robinson, landed upon the storm-beaten and inhospitable peninsula of Cape Cod, Captain Christopher

(5)

Newport, accompanied by that daring navigator, Bartholomew Gosnold, the discoverer of Capes Ann and Cod, in 1602, and that indomitable explorer, John Smith, sighted the capes of the Chesapeake Bay, and on May 13, 1607, under the patent of the London Company granted 1606, and in the name of their sovereign, James, planted and named after him the settlement of **James-town**, on the James river.

While the banks of the James gave birth to the first English settlement on the continent of North America, the Potomac, the other great tributary of the Chesapeake, gave birth to the immortal Washington, the commander-in-chief of the armies of the Rebellion against a tyrannous king, and the first President of the United States of America. Here also repose the mortal remains of this great patriot. Near its shores also rest the ashes of Patrick Henry, whose fiery eloquence struck the key-note of hostility to the encroachments of kingly despotism ; of Jefferson, the author of the Declaration of Independence ; of Peyton Randolph, President of the First Continental Congress ; of Edmund Randolph, the framer of the original draft of the Constitution of the United States (1787) ; of Madison and Monroe ; and, to cap the climax of this remarkable chain of events, upon its shores stands the Capital of this nation of millions of human creatures who trace the foundations of the civil and religious liberty which they now enjoy back to the principles enunciated and established by these heroic men, aided by their compeers of New England.

The object of this little companion is to bring to his attention as he glides along over the watery way, in a sort of panoramic progression, everything of interest in history, art, and nature, feeling that in no way can the traveller more profitably add to the pleasures of his journey.

The compiler wishes to express his deep sense of appreciation of the invaluable assistance rendered him by the Coast and Geodetic Survey of the United States in the preparation of the body of this work. The superior engravings of this work are by H. H. Nichols, of Washington.   DEB. R. K.

Washington, D. C.,1881.

INTRODUCTORY INFORMATION.

Travelers and excursionists *departing* from Washington for points on the POTOMAC RIVER, the CHESAPEAKE BAY, or JAMES RIVER, have a choice of a number of first-class steamers leaving on stated days.

Steamers.—The *principal lines* are the INLAND AND SEABOARD STEAMBOAT and the POTOMAC STEAMBOAT COMPANIES for *Potomac River Landings*, making connections at *Norfolk* with an old-established line of *ocean-steamers*. ; the POTOMAC TRANSPORTATION COMPANY, plying between Washington, Alexandria, and Baltimore; the CLYDE LINE between Washington, Philadelphia, Providence, and Boston; the UPPER POTOMAC STEAMBOAT COMPANY to river landings; the MOUNT VERNON boat, leaving daily at 10 a. m., and returning at 3:30 p. m., having the exclusive right of landing visitors at the home and tomb of Washington; and the POTOMAC FERRY COMPANY, hourly during the day between Washington and Alexandria.

The days and hours of departure are announced in the newspapers.

Fares.—The *rates* of passage by all these lines are very reasonable, and during the excursion season are placed at figures, and for a length of time, extremely advantageous to travelers and excursionists.

Hotels.—At all points accommodations may be had by those who wish to land, but it would be well beforehand to make inquiries of an officer of the steamer. At principal points patronized by travelers, the hotel accommodations are generally excellent and charges reasonable. Special rates can be had by those spending some time.

Summer Resorts.—Every year available points on the Potomac River and Chesapeake Bay are being occupied by enterprising parties for the enjoyment of the inhabitants of Washington during the heated term. Of late years the older places have been refitted and new ones added. It is now no longer necessary for citizens of Washington to travel to distant mountains, fashionable watering places or springs, for comfort or pleasure, as the Capital has its own summer places, within the means and easy access of those of moderate circumstances.

(7)

Fishing.—The Potomac is celebrated for the excellence of its fish. *Shad* and *Herring* are the principal seine fish. Seining is one of the leading industries of the river. During the summer, fall, and winter months, those fond of piscatorial sports find ample opportunity to indulge themselves with rod and line in pursuit of the *White Perch, Black Bass,* and *Rock.* The latter have been caught weighing one hundred and fifty pounds. In May and August *Sturgeon* also abound, and have been taken as high as the Little Falls. *Winter Shad* and *Carp* also abound in the proper season. "*Plank Shad*" excursions from Washington to the fishing grounds on the lower river are a favorite recreation for residents of the Capital during the spring and early summer months.

Game.—The Water Fowl of the Potomac have a world-wide renown. These comprise the most delicious of all game, the *Canvas Back,* and its close competitors for popularity, the *Red Head* and *Black Head* ducks. These, belonging to the drift fowl, congregate in large numbers in the middle of the river, and feed in deep water by diving, and may be seen from the steamers. The *Blue* and *Green Wing Teal, Mallard, Black Duck,* and *Widgeon,* all marsh fowls, are seen near the shores, feeding on wild oats, and abound during September and October. The *Swan* and *Wild Goose* of the Potomac, also drift fowls, are also famous. arriving in October and November, and leaving in March. The young swan is considered a great delicacy in the markets of Washington. In former years the drift and marsh fowl were taken by hunters in the vicinity of Washington, but are now never found in any numbers above Mount Vernon. The swan never approaches nearer than the Occoquan, about thirty miles below Washington, and thence to near the mouth of the river. The only water fowl which breeds on the Potomac is the *Summer Duck;* the rest are migratory.

Those who indulge in hunting aquatic fowl, frequent the favorite resorts of this game, easily accessible by steamer.

The extensive marsh off Washington, and along the banks below, during the autumn months abounds in *Reed Birds* and *Ortolan,* which are "bagged" in large numbers by city sportsmen.

The Potomac and James Rivers,

THE CHESAPEAKE BAY,

AND AN

Ocean Voyage to the Northern Cities.

We suppose the reader to have acquainted himself with the numerous and varied attractions of Washington, the governing city of the nation. No other city in the country possesses so much to interest and instruct the visitor. Here is the *Capitol*, with its massive architectural proportions and mighty iron dome ; its vast and magnificent

THE CAPITOL OF THE UNITED STATES OF AMERICA.

Legislative Halls, its libraries, bronze and marble staircases, sumptuous apartments and richly-gilded anterooms, beautiful statuary, paintings and frescoes ; the

(9)

Executive Mansion, the official home of the chief magistrate of the people, with its elegant *salons* and conservatories; the various *Executive Buildings*, with their imposing and symmetrical exteriors, and the many objects of interest within; its numerous *statues*, in marble and bronze, to departed greatness; its beautiful *parks*, with fountains and flowers; its majestic *avenues* and streets; its *galleries of art*; its *public libraries* and *institutions of science*; its palatial *private residences*; and indeed, everything necessary to the capital city of a mighty nation, and calculated to attract the senses and elevate and enlighten the mind.

To those who desire a complete historical and descriptive account of the city and its surroundings, see KEIM'S HANDBOOK OF WASHINGTON AND ITS ENVIRONS, a work compiled with great care and profusely illustrated, and designed not only as a guide to the city, for immediate use, but an entertaining work for home reading, and worthy of a conspicuous place in the library for future reference.

THE POTOMAC RIVER.

The **Potomac River**, which forms nearly the entire boundary between West Virginia and Virginia on the south, and Maryland on the north, has its fountain sources in two branches, the *Northern* rising on the eastern slopes of the Allegheny mountains, near the sources of the Cheat and Youghiogheny branches of the Monongahela, in the northern part of West Virginia; and the *Southern* in the Shenandoah range about the centre of the same state. The *North Branch* runs northeast from its source, forming the boundary between Allegheny county, Maryland, and Grant and Mineral counties, West Virginia, and has a course of one hundred and ten miles. The *South Branch*, one hundred and forty miles long, drains Pendleton county, West Virginia, and taking a northeasterly course, traverses the counties of Hardy and Hampshire. These two branches unite in Hampshire county, Maryland, about fifteen miles southeast of Cumberland, in that state. As far as HANCOCK, a station and post village on the Baltimore and Ohio railroad, it takes a somewhat irregular course towards the northeast, and thence swings off to the southeast as far as historic Harper's Ferry. Here the noble stream rolls in majestic grandeur through a wild gorge in the Blue Ridge range. The towering and precipitous walls, giddy mountain altitudes, and the rushing waters, constitute a landscape for sublimity and bold effects unexcelled on the Atlantic slope.

THE PRESIDENT'S HOUSE.

At **Harper's Ferry**, the river intersects the boundary between West Virginia and Virginia. Just east of the Blue Ridge, the picturesque Shenandoah, its principal tributary, falls into the Potomac. Thence to its mouth, the river divides Virginia and Maryland, taking a southeasterly direction. The fine scenery continues, sometimes bold and mountainous, and then again open and picturesque, receiving on the way the contributions of its principal affluents—the Kacapon, the Monocacy, and the Conecocheague rivers. The river thence sweeps by CUMBERLAND, an important industrial and business centre in the heart of a rich mining and agricultural district, and has all the characteristics of a mountain stream. There is a difference of twelve hundred feet between Westport and Washington. The descents in some places form picturesque *cascades*, the principal of which are the Shenandoah, Seneca, Great and Little Falls.   Released from the mountains, and passing through the narrow channel between Georgetown and Analostan Island, the river spreads out into a broad and magnificent estuary, beginning in front of Washington, and extending with a southwesterly trend seventy miles, and thence southeasterly to the Chesapeake Bay, and from two to seven miles wide.   From its mountain springs to its mouth in the Chesapeake Bay, latitude 38° north, the distance is four hundred miles, and as far as Washington the river is navigable for vessels drawing twenty-two feet of water.

EXCURSION I.

From Washington to the Great Falls of the Potomac.

DISTANCES.

FROM GEORGETOWN TO THE

	Miles.			Miles.
FEEDER LOCK	4	SEVEN LOCKS (UPPER)	. . .	8¾
LOCK NO. 2	4¼	SIX LOCKS (LOWER)	. . . .	12¾
MAGAZINE LOCK	5¾	" " (UPPER) GREAT		
SEVEN LOCKS (LOWER)	7¼	FALLS	. . . .	14

Hotel.—At the Upper Lock of the Falls of the Potomac, accommodations substantial, a good meal or lunch, may be had by those not provided with their own, at a reasonable price. Fishing tackle can be purchased at the store in the Hotel.

In the summer season a small *steam pleasure boat* makes frequent trips to the Great Falls of the Potomac.

GEORGETOWN AND AQUEDUCT OF THE ALEXANDRIA CANAL.

The *steamer* usually starts from its moorings on the canal between Congress and High streets, and may be conveniently reached by the Pennsylvania avenue horse cars, alighting at Congress street, and going south but a short distance. Usual fare for the round trip, 75 cents.

(13)

The days of departure of the boat are announced in the newspapers. Some seasons the steamer has made regular trips on Sundays, starting between 8 and 9 a. m., and returning by 6 p. m. Excursionists frequently make the trip to the Great Falls on one of the numerous canal boats leaving Georgetown for Cumberland during the week, and sometimes remain at the Falls from Saturday till Monday. Permission can be obtained from the boatmen. Owing to the locks, sixteen in number, to be passed going and returning, the trip requires from three to four hours each way.

To those desirous of enjoying a day of release from the restraints of life in the Executive Departments, or from everyday affairs, an excursion to the Great Falls affords everything that could be desired in the way of beauty of scenery ; in the proper season, fine fishing ; or in experiencing the novelty of canal navigation and locking over the elevations above the level line.

Leaving its moorings, the little steamer passes under a massive *arched bridge*, part of the original work of the canal.

On the east wall are inscriptions—north of the arch, "Andrew Jackson, President of the United States," "Charles F. Mercer, President of the Chesapeake and Ohio Canal," and names of the first directors ; " Built 1834," on the keystone, " O. H. Dibble, Builder ; " and on the south side of the arch, " Thomas F. Purcell, Superintending Engineer," and the names of his assistants. Over the keystone on the west side of the bridge are inscriptions, "John Cox, Mayor of Georgetown," "James Dunlop, Recorder."

As the boat proceeds, it passes by the immense *coal chutes*, from which the coal from the Cumberland mines is taken out of the canal boats, and transferred to the large three and four-masted schooners. in which it is carried to all parts of the Atlantic coast. A short distance beyond is the northern *entrance* to the *aqueduct* of the *Alexandria Canal*, incorporated 1830, where it crosses the Potomac. The *aqueduct* is 1,400 feet long, 40 feet wide, and 36 feet above high water. The stone piers are embedded 17 feet in the bed of the river, to resist the weight of ice from the river above. (See page 13.)

To this point, the *Georgetown Channel* of the Potomac, from forty to sixty feet deep, and *Analostan or Mason's Island*, seventy acres, once the residence of Gen. John Mason, Commissary General of Prisoners in the war of 1812, and the birthplace of J. M. Mason, Confederate Commissioner to Europe, may be seen on the left, with the houses of Georgetown rising precipitously on the right.

Passing the aqueduct, the canal skirts the banks of the river. The forest-clad cliffs opposite are in Virginia, and it was at the foot of these that John Randolph, of Roanoke, and Henry Clay, fought their celebrated duel. The massive stone and brick buildings, with their lofty bell-towers, crowning the picturesque summit on the right, are the *Georgetown University*, under the care of the Fathers of the Society of Jesus, founded in 1789, raised to a university in 1815, and the oldest Roman Catholic college in the country. As the boat steams along, at a distance of one and a half miles, the embankment of the *Distributing Reservoir* of the Washington aqueduct may be seen on the crest of the ridge on the right. From this point the immense iron *mains*, which convey the supply of water into Washington, begin. Here also ends the nine-foot cylindrical *conduit* which carries the water from the Great Falls into the receiving and distributing reservoirs. A short distance beyond, the *Receiving Reservoir* appears in sight on the hill on the right.

After pursuing a level of four miles from Georgetown, we arrive at the

Feeder Lock.—Before reaching, but near this lock, is the site of the celebrated chain bridge, now replaced by a modern structure. On the right, commanding the bridge, stood Battery Martin Scott, one of the defences of Washington in 1861–65. In the earliest days, this was the only crossing of the Potomac in this vicinity, except the ferry at Georgetown, between Maryland and Virginia. In 1811, a chain suspension bridge was erected over the stream, but was carried away in a freshet and ice-gorge. The present iron bridge (a Howe truss) was built in 1870. It is 1,350 feet long. At this point may also be seen the *rocky channel* of the *Little Falls of the Potomac.* The waters of the river, which have been sweeping along with majestic and swelling flood towards the broad estuary below, here rush and roar amidst boulders of rugged form and immense size. The *scenery* is romantic beyond description, and will inspire the admiration of every lover of nature. From the tranquil current above to the quiet flood below the distance is one and a half miles, and the fall thirty-seven feet.

After making the rise of the *Feeder Lock*, and following a one-fourth-mile level,

Lock No. 2 is reached.

At the end of the next level, one and a half miles, **Magazine Lock** is reached, so named after an old government magazine which stood here at the time. Near here the valley of *Cabin John Creek* will be seen. Across this deep, narrow, and rugged fissure in the hills, and within sight of the canal, springs the famous *Cabin John Bridge*, which carries the Washington aqueduct over the valley. This bridge has the largest single span arch of masonry in the world, being 220 feet spring, 57½ feet from the

CABIN JOHN BRIDGE.

springing line, 101 feet above the creek, and constructed of granite and Seneca stone. It is 420 feet long, and cost $237,000. The Grosvenor Bridge over the river Dee at Chester, England, is 200 feet span.

The steamer, after traversing another level of one and a half miles, reaches the

Seven Locks.—Here will be afforded an opportunity to get off and take a stroll along the tow-path, and, at the same time, to watch the process of locking to a higher summit. These seven locks are within a distance of about one and a half miles, and the total rise is 56 feet. The locks are constructed of solid masonry, 100 feet long, 15 feet wide, and 8 feet lift.

Leaving the Seven Locks, the canal makes another level of four miles, when the

Six Locks are reached. These are the same size as the seven locks. The scenery by this time is rugged and wild. The gently undulating outlying mountain-spurs, with cultivated fields on the Maryland side, have ended, and forests of evergreen and deciduous trees have taken their places.

At the last of the Six Locks is the HOTEL, and the terminus of the trip. The passengers here disembark, and dispose themselves for recreation as their inclinations prompt. The boat will lie here for four or five hours. It is customary for excursionists to cross the canal and stroll over to the falls, and ramble there under the shade of rugged oaks, birch and jessamine, or among the rocks which lie around in wild grandeur. The *Potomac* at this point narrows to one hundred yards in width, and

THE GREAT FALLS OF THE POTOMAC.

makes a descent of eighty feet, in a series of cataracts and falls, in a distance of one and a half miles. The greatest single leap is forty feet. The river here divides into *two channels*, the Maryland and Virginia, separated by Conn's and Great Falls islands. Across the Maryland channel a *supply dam* of solid masonry, with *gate-houses* and *gates*, has been thrown, which will be extended to the Virginia side if necessary to increase the water supply of the Capital. At this point also the water of the river is turned into the nine-foot conduit, which begins here.

The Government owns five acres at the falls to control the water-right. The capacity of the aqueduct, a nine-foot conduit, is eighty million gallons in twenty-four hours.

The *scenery* here is weird and wild. The immense rocks lying about in immense masses present a scene of the wildest confusion. Forest trees, and a dense undergrowth of wild shrubbery, grow upon the shores, and in the summer time adorn the stern face of nature with luxuriant foliage.

The *Falls* are also a popular resort for fishermen in the spring and fall, when the black bass resort there in great numbers, and the captivating angler's sport presents increased temptations.

The Potomac was early an object of *improvement*. George Washington conceived the idea of connecting the waters of the Potomac and the Ohio by a system of canals and slack-water navigation. He made several reconnoissances of the river, and a survey and soundings of the stream from Georgetown to beyond the Great Falls. This scheme was engaging his attention when he was called to the command of the armies of the Revolution, 1776-83, and after the close of the war he again enlisted himself in the prosecution of this work.

The Potomac Company, chartered by the State of Maryland in 1784, completed a canal before 1800, around the Little and Great Falls. These efforts were followed by the charters by Congress, and the States of Maryland, Pennsylvania, and Virginia, of the present enterprise. Work was commenced in 1828. The object was the connection of tide-water on the Potomac with the head of navigation on the Ohio, a distance of 360 miles. In 1841 the canal was opened to Cumberland, 182 miles, at a cost of $13,000,000, of which Maryland subscribed $5,000,000, the United States $1,000,000, Washington $1,000,000, and Georgetown, Alexandria, and Virginia, each $250,000. Cumberland remains the terminus. The execution of the enterprise was a work of great difficulty. There are 75 locks of 100 feet in length, 15 feet in width, and averaging 8 feet lift, 11 aqueducts crossing the Monocacy river, consisting of 7 arches of 54 feet span; also 190 culverts of various dimensions, some sufficiently spacious to admit of the passage of wagons. The canal is fed by a number of dams across the Potomac, varying from 500 to 800 feet in length, and from 4 to 20 feet elevation. The breadth of the canal is 60 feet for the first 60 miles above Georgetown, and for the remaining distance to Cumberland 50 feet, with a uniform depth of 6 feet. The entire lift is about 600 feet. The aqueducts, locks, and culverts, are constructed of stone, laid in hydraulic cement. The *tunnel* through the "Pawpaw Ridge" is 3,118 feet in length, and 24 feet in diameter, with an elevation of 17 feet clear of the surface of the water. The canal connects with Rock creek. The canal to Cumberland opens the immensely valuable and rich coal sections of western Maryland and West Virginia. The unfinished portion of the canal, from Cumberland to Pittsburgh, is 178 miles.

The hour for the *return* of the boat having arrived, ample warning is given by blowing the whistle. All being again aboard, the boat starts on her homeward voyage, reversing the order of things, and dropping down the step-like locks until the long level leading back into Georgetown is reached.

EXCURSION II.

THE POTOMAC RIVER,

From the City of Washington to its Mouth.

DISTANCE FROM WASHINGTON

TO MOUTH OF POTOMAC RIVER (PT. LOOK-
OUT) . . . . 106 Miles.
TO BALTIMORE . . . . 190 "
TO OLD PT. COMFORT (FORTRESS MONROE) 183 "
TO NORFOLK . . . . 194 "

TABLE OF DISTANCES TO POINTS

On the Potomac River, compiled by the United States
Coast and Geodetic Survey.

FROM WASHINGTON TO

	Miles.		Miles.
Alexandria	5	Maryland Point	45
Rosier's Bluff	8	Nanjemoy Creek	52
Broad Creek	9	Upper Cedar Point Light . .	53
Fort Washington	12	Mathias Point	55
Mount Vernon	14	Persimmon Point	59
Marshall Point	15	Lower Cedar Point Light . .	61½
White House	16½	Rosier's Creek	64
Hollowing Point	20	Monroe's Creek	68
Craney Island	21	Pope's Creek.	72
Glymont	22	Great Wicomico Bay	75
Indian Head	23½	Blackiston's Island Light . .	79
Mattawoman Creek	27½	Machadock River	85
Cockpit Point	29	Ragged Point	87
Quantico Creek	31	Piney Point	89
Sandy Point.	34	St. Mary's River	99
Liverpool Point	36	Point Lookout Light . . .	106
Smith's Point	39	Smith Point Lightships . .	119
Aquia Creek	39½		

At the foot of *Seventh street* west, reached by the
Seventh or *Ninth Street Horse Railways*, going south; or
at *Georgetown*, conveniently reached by the *Pennsylvania
Avenue* or *F Street Horse Railways*, going west, the traveler takes one of the many palatial steamers plying to
points on the Potomac River and the Chesapeake Bay,
preparatory to a voyage not only replete with interest and
information, but unrivaled in everything which contri-
butes to his safety and comfort.

Seated on the deck awaiting the departure of the steamer, which perhaps is already showing signs of life by the pulsations of the mighty machinery in the depths of the hold, the impatient hissing of steam, and the general stir on deck, may be seen the long line of *water front* of Washington ; the lofty dome of the *Capitol*; and the bold outlines of the mighty *public edifices*, mingling with the mass of private structures, and the buildings of

ARLINGTON.

Georgetown nestling amid the distant hills on the right beyond, and historic *Arlington* crowning the summit of the wooded elevation on the Virginia side of the river.

Or, again, seated on the deck of the steamer at *Georgetown*, the port of entry of Washington, will be observed the *shipping* of the city, the immense *chutes* and *wharves* at which the bituminous coal from the fields of West Virginia, brought down by canal, is being loaded on schoon-

VIEW OF WASHINGTON FROM THE POTOMAC.

THE MOUTH OF THE ANACOSTIA RIVER (21).

ers for transportation to ports on the Atlantic seaboard ; and beyond, through the narrow portals of the hills, may be seen the waters of the Potomac coming down from the eastern declivities of the Appalachian chain, and around a scene of picturesque beauty, precipitous cliffs, wooded hills, and the water-fringed, romantic isle of Analostan.

Starting at Georgetown, where the river channel is five hundred yards wide and forty to sixty feet deep, the *fairway* of the stream runs close to the Virginia bank. The mass of buildings of the city with a few distinctive objects may be seen. Between this channel and the Washington shore is an expansive *marsh* of about 1,000 acres,

THE UNITED STATES BARRACKS.

one-third clear at low water. Passing the *Draw* of the *Long Bridge*, where the stream is nearly one mile wide, the steamer heads for *Giesboro Point*.

Or starting at Washington, and passing down along the river front of the city, the steamer first comes to the long wooded peninsula upon which is situated the

United States Barracks, established in 1881, formerly the United States Arsenal, latitude 38° 51′ 51″ N., longitude 77° 00′ 43″ West of Greenwich.

The *grounds* are about twelve feet above high water. The *peninsula* is formed by the Potomac river, and the Anacostia or Eastern Branch, and was first known as Greenleaf's Point. A *military station* was established here in

1803 ; shops erected in 1807 ; powder stored here in 1812 ; was a regular depot of supplies 1813 ; was destroyed by the British 1814 ; rebuilt in 1815 ; and was a depot of ordnance supplies during the Rebellion, 1861-65. The total size of the *Reservation*, including the purchase of 1857, is sixty-nine acres. There are *officers' quarters*, barracks for men, guard-house, offices, storehouses, magazines, stables, hospitals, machine and blacksmith shops, laundries, etc., for five batteries. The bodies of Booth and the other conspirators in the assassination of President Lincoln were first buried here, as also Wirz, the Andersonville prison-keeper.

After running close to the barracks grounds for three-fourths of a mile to *Greenleaf's Point*, the steamer opens the

Anacostia River, or *Eastern Branch* of the Potomac, as it is locally called. This stream runs in a north-easterly direction from the main river to historic *Bladensburg*, the scene of many famous duels, some six

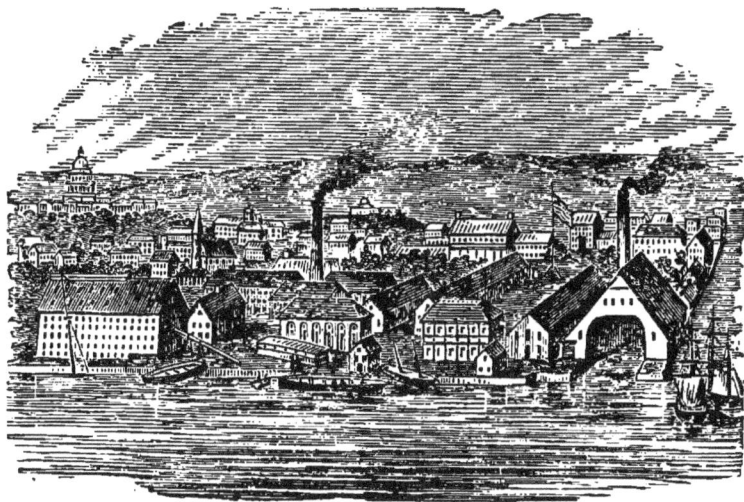

THE NAVY YARD.

miles above. The *Anacostia* is three-fourths of a mile wide at its mouth, but has a very narrow channel, running close under the Washington bank. At the *Anacostia bridge*, one and one-half miles above *Greenleaf's Point*, the Branch is only five hundred yards wide. As soon as we open the river, we see the *United States Navy Yard*—the two ship-houses forming conspicuous objects —and generally several war vessels lying in the stream. The *navy-yard*, established in 1804, is on the north bank of the Anacostia, one and one-fourth miles from *Green-*

leaf's Point, and occupies an area of about twenty-seven acres. It is now used mainly as a construction-yard, and for experiments in ordnance and gunnery. The frigates Brandywine—forty-four guns, Minnesota, and other famous war vessels, were built here ; and it was from this place that the sloop of war Pensacola started on her memorable run down the river in 1862, when the banks below Washington were lined with Confederate batteries at every available point. (See page 21.)

The little village opposite to the navy yard is *Union-town*—and the long dark red building on the hill with turrets which give it the appearance of a castle, is "*St. Elizabeth's*," the *United States Hospital for the Insane*. The southern point of entrance to Anacostia river is called

Giesboro' Point, and is easily recognized by the thick grove of trees on it, with a house peeping out from it, and a long wharf running out to the edge of the channel. At this point the Georgetown, Washington, and Anacostia channels unite and form the *broad channel*, which extends down the main stream. The *length* of the main channel from the Aqueduct at Georgetown to deep water off Giesboro' Point is four and two-thirds miles. The *depth* at mean high water, at the shoalest place below Washington, is twenty-two feet.

The *river channel* now keeps the eastern shore, running about south-southwest to *Alexandria*. After clearng Giesboro' Point, on the crest of the first hill on the left stood *Fort Carroll*, and the second *Fort Greble*, two earth-works commanding the river, and forming part of the cordon. of defences of Washington, 1861–65. The *Naval Magazine*, with its wharf, is also on the east bank, one and three-fourths miles below Giesboro' Point. The long *wharf of the Baltimore and Ohio Railroad Company* is directly opposite to the northern end of Alexandria. The wide, shallow creek, also opposite the city, is called *Oxon Creek*.

Alexandria, originally called *Belhaven*, is the seat of justice of the county of the same name in Virginia, and is a port of entry. It presents a commanding appearance from the river.

It early enjoyed a considerable *commercial* importance, carrying on trade with ports of the East and West Indies, and on our own coast. It is the emporium of the important fish trade of the Potomac. At one time it was the rival of Baltimore commercially. The river here is one mile wide, and thirty-four to fifty-four feet deep, affording commodious anchorage for vessels of the greatest draught. From here Braddock set out on his toilsome march to the fatal forests on the Monongahela. During the *Revolution*, 1776–82, it was regarded as a place of great strategic importance. The British General Gage in 1776 contemplated an overland attack from Pittsburgh, while the fleet of the Earl of Dunmore was to attack it from the river, and thus cut off communications between the northern and southern armies of the revolutionary colonies. The plan, however, was never carried out. During the *War of 1812* (Aug. 27, 1814), after Fort Washington had been abandoned and blown up, the British fleet moved up to Alexandria, which was saved from pillage and flames by the exertions of several prominent citizens, notably Edward Lloyd, the half-brother of the Marquis of Beckwith. The latter was with the fleet at the time. The British commander, while his fleet lay at anchor off the city, seized 16,000 barrels of flour, 1,000 hogsheads of tobacco, 150 bales of cotton, 3 ships, 3 brigs, and a large quantity of wines and cigars. The *city* possesses much *historic interest*. It was the home of *Lord Fairfax*, one of the ancient and noble English families settled in Virginia. His Lordship's

ALEXANDRIA FROM BELOW.

mansion still (1881) stands in excellent preservation. The *Christ Episcopal church*, commenced in 1765, and finished in 1773, of bricks imported from England, and still standing, was attended by General Washington when at his home at Mt. Vernon. Near the city is a *national cemetery*, in which lie the remains of 3,635 Union soldiers.

The delightful location of the city and its convenience of access from Washington, which lies in sight, has made it the place of *residence* of many business men and officials from the latter. Four *railroads* centre here; six regular lines of *steamers* touch here; and a *canal* connects with the Chesapeake and Ohio Canal at Georgetown. There are also some manufactures. The *population* in 1870 was 13,570, and 1880, 13,658.

The long, low, green point at the south end of Alexandria, with the light-house on it, is

Jones Point —It was to this point, April 15, 1791, that the municipal authorities of Alexandria, Va., and commissioners of the proposed federal city, in accordance with the proclamation of President Washington, March 30, 1791, announcing the *bounds* of the new Federal

Territory, provided for by national legislation under authority of the Constitution, proceeded and planted, according to the solemn rites of Masonry, the *initial or corner-stone* of the Federal Territory afterwards named the District of Columbia. The present light-house stands upon the *site* of these interesting ceremonies. In the beginning of the century it was proposed to erect a " *great fort* " on this point, to be called *Columbia*, in commemoration of this event.

The wide stream south is *Hunting Creek*.

The steep, wooded hill about one and one-fourth miles below Jones Point, and opposite, is *Rozier's Bluff*, on which stands

FORT FOOTE.

Fort Foote, Md., lat. 38° 46″ N., long. 77° 1′ 25″ West of Greenwich, named after Rear Admiral Andrew Hull Foote, U. S. Navy, the hero of the naval operations at Forts Henry, Donelson and Island No. 10, and commander of the South Atlantic Blockading Squadron.

The *fort* is about ninety feet above high water, on the left bank of the Potomac River, about eight miles below Washington. It was *established* in 1862, as one of the river defences of the Capital. The government took possession of the ground May 10, 1862. The southern part of the *Reservation*, containing 15 acres, 1 rood, 4½ perches, was *purchased* from F. W. Rosier ; the northern part, adjoining and containing 51 acres, 1 rood, 12¾ perches, from the heirs of Benedict Edelin. *Jurisdiction* over the land was ceded to the government by an act of the General Assembly of Maryland, approved April 1, 1872. The *fortification* is constructed of earth, and is held from the United States Barracks, Washington. It is in charge of a non-commissioned officer. In case of emergency the *garrison* could be increased to five companies of artillery. The *water* supply is ample.

About one and a half miles below *Rozier's Bluff*, and on the same bank, is *Broad Creek*, very shallow, but five-eighths of a mile wide at its mouth. The extent of marsh land opposite to Rozier's is known as the *Hell Hole.* The post hamlet of Collingwood, in Fairfax county, Virginia, is opposite and below Fort Foote. From Rozier's the gray walls of

Fort Washington, a stone casemated work, can be seen perched upon the bluff. It is two miles below Broad Creek, about four miles below Fort Foote, nearly six miles below Alexandria, and twelve below Washington. There is a *light-house* of open wood work on the end of the point.

Fort Washington, Maryland, lat. 30° 42′ 37″ N., long. 77° 48″ W., is *situated* on a bluff, about one hundred and twenty feet above high water, on he eastern bank of the Potomac River, where Piscataway creek, five-eighths if a mile wide and south of the fort, empties into it. It was *established* in 1808, as a *river defence* in the approach to Washington—the Government hen buying about four acres. The *present work* was built in 1815, five acres

FORT WASHINGTON.

more land being then purchased. Another *purchase* of 34 acres was made in 1833, and in 1875 a farm of 289 acres was added. The total *area* of the Reservation is 333 acres, 3 roods, 11 perches. *Jurisdiction* over the land wa ceded to the United States by an act of the General Assembly of Maryland approved April 11, 1874. The *supply* of water is good. The banks of th ravines are all well wooded. The trees east of the fort have grown up since 1865. The fort was built into the hill, with three tiers of *casemates* facing the river, and bringing the upper tier on a level with the top of the hill. A new *water battery* for guns of heavy calibre has been commenced. There are accommodations at the fort for a garrison of five batteries of artillery, with officers' quarters, kitchens, hospitals, magazines, etc.

While Ross, the British general, was moving upon Washington by land, a British *fleet* of two frigates, 36 and 38 guns ; two rocket ships, 18 guns each ; two bomb vessels, 8 guns each, and one schooner, under Commodore Gordon, moved up the Potomac. *Fort Washington* alone stood between the British and Alexandria and the Capital. Despite the efforts of the citizens of Alexandria, Washington, and Georgetown, nothing was done to strengthen their means of defence. Some fifty thousand dollars, loaned the government by the banks of Alexandria for the purpose of defence, was diverted to other uses. The garrison of Fort Washington consisted of but eighty men, under Captain Samuel T. Dyson, who had orders to be vigilant, and if threatened by land to

blow up the work and retreat across the river. On August 27, after the capture of Washington, the British squadron appeared, whereupon Dyson, in-
stead of defending it from the water front, as was intended, blew up the work
and fled without firing a gun. As a consequence, the enemy's squadron con-
tinued its cruise, and anchored off Alexandria the next day.

Fort Washington is *held* from the United States Barracks at Washington, and is in the charge of a non-commissioned officer. It is an extremely *interesting work*,
and is well worthy of a visit, especially to one not famil-
iar with warlike defences, as it gives a very good idea of
a sea-coast fort.

The wooded point on the western bank opposite Fort
Washington is *Sheridan's Point*. Here the river makes
its first bend—turning about west-southwest, and keeping that direction for about four miles to *Ferry Point*, on
the western side of Mt. Vernon.

MOUNT VERNON FROM THE RIVER.

Mt. Vernon, the home of Washington, lies on the
north bank of the river, between *Little Hunting Creek* on
the east, and *Doag Creek* on the west. The *house* is
about one and three-fourths miles below Sheridan's
Point, and is beautifully situated on the summit of a very
steep bluff, diversified with groves of trees and grassy

slopes. A *wharf* at the base of the bluff is the landing-place of the steamer which carires excursionists to and from the place. The *dwelling-house* is seen through the trees as you come abreast of Sheridan's Point. At Sheridan's the river is five-eighths of a mile wide, and at Mt. Vernon nearly one and one-fourth miles wide. The *wharf* at Mt. Vernon is exactly fourteen miles below Washington. *Mt. Vernon on the Potomac*, a post hamlet, is near the landing.

MOUNT VERNON FROM THE ALEXANDRIA ROAD.

The *mansion*, two stories high, ninety-six feet long, and surmounted by a cupola, is of wood, cut in imitation of stone. The centre was erected by Lawrence Washington, the General's brother, and the wings by the General himself. The *name* is after Admiral Vernon, in whose fleet Lawrence Washington, the original proprietor, served in colonial times. The *veranda* in the rear commands a fine view of the Potomac. The *vault* containing the remains of Washington is on the path leading from the landing to the mansion. The *home* and *grave* of Washington, after the demise of Judge Bushrod Washington in 1832, fell into decay. In 1856 the *Ladies' Mount Vernon Association of the United States purchased* the mansion and contiguous grounds, and have since restored them as nearly as possible to the condition in which their great occupant left them, and have added many articles of interest connected with his own life, or associated with the times in which he lived.

Doag Creek is one mile wide at its mouth, but quite shallow. It is said that Washington used to go ducking here, and that he made a careful detailed survey of it and sounded it out. Its eastern point of entrance is called *Ferry Point*, and directly opposite to it is *Marshall Point*, on the eastern bank of the Potomac, the site of **Marshall Hall,** a post village of Fairfax county, Va., and a noted summer-resort. The pavilion and buildings are plainly seen as the steamer passes. This part of the bank is cleared, cultivated, level country. There are also groves of ornamental trees surrounding the grounds.

At *Marshall Hall* the river begins a gradual *turn* to the southward, running first about southwest by south for about one and a half miles to abreast of *Whitestone Point*, and then south for three miles to abreast of *Hallowing Point*. *Whitestone Point* is on the west bank, two and a quarter miles below Ferry Point. It is a high, steep, wooded bluff, with yellow and white precipitous faces, having patches of scrub on them. A little over half a mile above it, and about two and five-eighths miles below Mt. Vernon wharf, is a long, low, white house, standing on the flat ground at the base of a precipitous, wooded hill. This is the **White House,** in Fairfax county, Va., once a famous summer-resort.

After the *surrender* of Alexandria, efforts were made by the Government to *capture or destroy* the British fleet in its descent of the Potomac. As the Maryland and District militia could not be rallied in time, Commodore Rodgers, who was ordered from Philadelphia to Washington to assist in the defense of the city, but too late to be of service, having had but time to reach Baltimore when Washington fell, was directed to hasten to the Potomac with all the available men he could gather. His force amounted to about 400 seamen, 50 marines, and four twelve-pounders. This force was commanded by Rodgers, Perry, Porter, and Creighton. Batteries were thrown up on the bank of the river at the "*White House*" and at *Indian Head*, where the river narrows, both on the Virginia side. Riflemen were stationed along the wooded banks between these points. Volunteers from Washington also planted batteries on the bank. By September 1, the British found themselves cut off. The forces on shore grew stronger every day by fresh accessions of guns from Washington and militia from the surrounding country. For several days there were at intervals some brisk engagements between the Americans on shore and the British on the river.

Finally, matters growing serious, the British opened a concentrated fire of ten vessels, some one hundred and seventy-three guns, upon Porter's battery at the White House, and hurled such a fire of shot upon it as to silence it. This disposed of Perry's battery at Indian Head was in turn attacked. The guns commanded by Lieutenant George C. Read did effective service, but the superior numbers and weight of metal of the enemy silenced them also. The British with their plunder thence proceeded unobstructed to the Chesapeake.

On the south side of *Whitestone Point* is *Gunston Cove*, three-fourths of a mile wide, but shallow. It runs to the northwestward for a mile and a quarter, where it receives the waters of two shallow creeks, *Accotink* and

Pohtick. On the south bank is *Gunston* Post-office, in Fairfax county, Va.

On Pohtick or Poheek creek, seven miles south of Mount Vernon, in a forest of oak, chestnut, and pines, stands an ancient, crumbling church edifice, built of stone, with a hip roof, and of considerable size. Here George Washington was a parishioner, and frequently attended divine service, its rector at that time being Rev. Mason L. Weems, Washington's first biographer. The pulpit was a superior piece of workmanship. The *Poheick Protestant Episcopal church*, named after the river so named by the Indians, was in Truro parish. In 1764 the old church had fallen into decay. There was much discussion as between the old and a new site. Washington favored the new site on the Poheick. Most of the parishioners favored the old, but Washington at the meeting presenting a map showing the convenience of the new location, it was accepted, and in 1765 the new church was built. Washington was a vestryman in Truro and Fairfax parishes, at Poheick and Alexandria. The Masons and Fairfaxes also worshiped here.

INDIAN HEAD.

At *Whitestone Point* the river is a mile wide, but at *Gunston's Cove* it spreads out to one and three-quarters miles, but soon contracts again to one and one-eighth at *Hallowing Point.* The two points which mark the lower end of this southerly reach are *Hollis' Point* on the east bank, and *Hallowing Point* on the west. The former is low, flat, and marshy; the latter abrupt, precipitous, and thickly-wooded. On the south side of Hollis' Point makes in *Pamunkey Creek*, small, narrow, and shallow. Here the river again turns, this time nearly west southwest for nearly three and three-fourth miles to High Point, the eastern point of entrance to *Occoquan Creek*. The river widens to over two miles in the middle of this reach, and then gradually contracts again, being only one and a quarter miles at

Indian Head.—This remarkable headland is visible as

soon as you open the reach, and appears on the left bank as a high, densely-wooded bluff with perpendicular faces, showing here and there the yellow sand. (See *White House* for engagement here in 1814.) *High Point*, on the opposite bank, is a high, steep bluff, with sandy faces, and its top crowned with a dense growth of trees. In the middle of the reach, about three-fourths of a mile from Hallowing Point, will be seen *Craney Island*, a very small, low, flat islet. The channel passes on its eastern side, and you cannot go close to it on account of the flats surrounding it. The left bank, from the Pamunkey to *Chapman's Point* (opposite to Craney Island), presents a beautiful appearance in summer, the country being nearly all cleared and cultivated, and of an undulating or slightly rolling character, the swales gradually getting higher as they are more distant from the bank. What houses are seen stand at the bases of the high grounds. Just below *Chapman's Point*, perpendicular bluffs begin, and extend to *Indian Head*. These cliffs are quite high, and their sides are in some places clothed with trees, and in other places show bare, yellow, sandy faces, descending precipitously to the water.

Glymont, a post village of Charles county, Maryland, about a mile below Chapman's Point, is a well-known watering-place, and is situated on a high perpendicular wooded bluff, with cliff-like faces. There are two wharves here, and groups of white houses at the base of the cliffs. The large white house on top of the hill is very conspicuous. At Glymont you are exactly twenty-two miles below Washington.

Opposite to *Indian Head*, on the right or north bank of the river, and a little over two miles below *Hallowing Point*, is *Sycamore Point*, with cultivated, slightly undulating country, diversified with groves of trees, and showing in places steep, sandy banks.

Occoquan River is nearly two and a half miles wide at its mouth, while the river is only one and three-eighths miles, and the creek is therefore likely to be mistaken for the river by strangers in coming from below. The course, however, will determine—the river running east-northeast, and the creek due north. Though so wide, Occoquan is shoal, not more than six feet in the best channel being found beyond High Point. Its western

point of entrance, called *Freestone Point*, is quite
easily recognized, being a high, steep bluff, wooded head,
cleared in some places, with perpendicular, cliff-like face.
A post hamlet of Fairfax county, Virginia, named
Freestone, on the Alexandria and Fredericksburg railroad, stands on the south side of the cove. At *Freestone
Point*, during the war, were *Confederate batteries*, and
many brisk engagements took place between these and
those at *Cockpit Point* below, and the *Potomac flotilla*,
under the brave commander Ward, in one of which engagements he lost his life. (*at Aquia Creek*

Occoquan, established by act of Assembly of Virginia
in 1804, is a post-village of Prince William county, Va.,

THE POSSUM NOSE. (SEE P. 35).

and a place of considerable local importance. The
county was established in 1730. In 1835, Occoquan had
a cotton manufactory running one thousand spindles, one
of the first erected in the state. The town lies six miles
above the mouth of the river. *Woodbridge*, a post-village lower down the Occoquan, is at the crossing of the
Alexandria and Fredericksburg railroad. It has several
churches, a bank, etc. Population, two hundred and
twenty-eight. The *Occoquan River* here has a fall of
seventy-two feet in one and a half miles, affording fine
water power for several mills. The country in the
vicinity is very picturesque.

Lord Dunmore, the last of the royal governors of Virginia, driven from
Gwyn's Island in July, 1776, his place of refuge, with a force of whites and negroes devastated the shores of the Potomac, carrying his revengeful expedi-
tion as far as the destruction of the famous mills at Occoquan. It is said that
his dastardly purpose was to destroy Mt. Vernon and to capture Lady Washington. The sturdy sons of Prince William county, however, enraged at the

outrages of this last vestige of royalty in the colony, armed and rallied for defence; and after some brisk encounters on the river-shores in this vicinity, drove the fugitive governor to his ships and compelled him to fall back into the bay.

The waters about the mouth of the Occoquan are the favorite *feeding* haunts of the *swan*, it being the spawning ground of the white shad. This noble bird also frequents the river for a distance of forty miles below. In early days the swan resorted hither in flocks of several hundred, and might be seen floating gracefully on the waters, their white plumage at a distance resembling the driven snow, and in the evenings their sonorous notes could be heard for several miles. Their size was immense, sometimes measuring six feet from bill to toe, and eight feet from tip to tip. The swan remains in the river during the entire winter.

The small creek making in on the north side of *Freestone Point* is *Neabsico*, and that on its south side *Powell's Creek*. Neither is of importance. Seen from below the bluff, *Freestone Point* is smaller and more abrupt than from above—the land being low until the base of the bluff is reached, when it rises with a nearly perpendicular slope to the summit. The river is here two miles and a half wide, with the channel close under the left bank. *Deep Point*, on the eastern or left bank, is directly opposite *Freestone Point*, and nearly three and a half miles below *Indian Head*. It is a yellow sand bluff, with perpendicular faces, clothed with small trees and patches of scrub. On its south side makes in *Mattawoman Creek*, which although nearly a mile wide at its mouth, has a depth of not more than six feet at low tide, and is remarkable only as being a famous *shad and herring fishery*.

Fisheries.—The fisheries of the Potomac constitute an important and remunerative industry, and give employment to a large fleet of vessels, and not less than ten thousand men. The Potomac *shad fisheries* rank with the largest in the United States, and during the spring months the voyager will see the immense nets, some a mile in length, stretching out into the river. They bring in large numbers of the finny delicacy at a haul. *Planked shad* or *shad-bakes* are among the notable attractions of numerous excursions from Washington to points below the White House.

The *herring fisheries* also rank foremost in this branch of industry in the United States, and in quality this fish is rivalled only by the delicate herring of Nova Scotia. Immense quantities of this valuable fish of commerce are cured on the river, and shipped to ports in the United States and the West Indies.

Two miles below *Occoquan* formerly stood the ancient town of *Colchester*, prominent in colonial times, but of which no traces are now left.

Stumpy Point, on the southwestern side of Mattawoman creek, is one of the principal so-called "*landings*," that is places for landing the huge nets, and has nothing to especially distinguish it, being of moderate height and fringed with low trees and scrub. It is directly opposite to *Cockpit Point*, on the right bank of the river. This point (Cockpit), famous during the blockade of the Potomac, is two and one-fourth miles below Freestone Point, and seen from the river appears like a high, round bluff; but it is in reality low, level, and fringed with trees, while the bluff appearance is given by the

Possum Nose, (See p. 33) a round, wooded head, about one-fourth of a mile below the point, and the site of the Confederate batteries which did so much damage during the Rebellion, 1861–65. The river is only a little over a mile wide between *Stumpy and Cockpit Points*. It was here that *Capt. Ward* was killed. A little over a mile below *Stumpy Point*, on the left bank, is the entrance to

QUANTICO.

Chicomuxen Creek, on the south side of which is the landing known as *Budd's Ferry*. All of this shore is devoted during the season to shad fishery. On the right bank opposite to the Ferry, and over two miles below Cockpit Point, is the mouth of

Quantico Creek.—There are nine feet at low water in the creek, and the banks are partly cleared, and have several warehouses and dwellings on them. A deep cut, made by the wagon road leading over the bluff behind, is very noticeable, as is also the large wharf just below *Shipping Point*, the southern point of the creek's mouth. *Shipping Point* is a little over thirty-one miles from Washington.

Quantico (Potomac City) near the mouth of the Quan-

tico Creek, a post village of Prince William county, Va.,
is at the crossing of the *Richmond, Fredericksburg, and
Potomac Railroad*, which here connects with the *Alexandria and Fredericksburg road*.

The course of the river from *Indian Head* to *Shipping
Point* is very nearly southwest, but it now turns about
south, and gradually widens until at *Lower Thom's
Point*, directly opposite to *Potomac Creek*, and ten miles
below Budd's Ferry, it is three miles wide. The deep
channel runs close under the left bank all the way.
There is nothing remarkable on either bank until you
come to

Aquia Creek, (See p. 37) nine miles below Quantico.
This place, famous during the war as a great army depot,
is now almost deserted, but is easily recognized by the
long railroad wharf, with warehouses and depot on its
south bank. Its northern point of entrance is called
Brent's Point, and is also sufficiently remarkable, being a
sandy point, with tall, ragged-looking and very conspicuous trees on it, and a tall, narrow-fronted dwelling-house
near by. The south side of the creek, except w ere the
railroad buildings are, is all marsh for half a mile back,
when high, sandy, wooded hills begin. *Aquia Creek*, a
post village of Stafford county, Va., is the terminus of a
short branch of the *Richmond and Potomac railroad*,
which connects with the *Alexandria and Fredericksburg
road*, and is a little over forty miles from Washington.

It was near here that the government purchased *quarries* in 1792, and took
out the freestone from which the Executive Mansion and old portions of the
Capitol were built. The stone was then shipped to Washington on flat-boats
and schooners. A church built in 1750 is in the village, and freestone of excellent quality is still the chief article of export. The *county* of Stafford was
created by act of Assembly, 1675.

Nearly opposite *Aquia Creek*, on the left bank, is
Smith's Point, covered with bushes and low scrub, and
having a small wharf and warehouse at the base of the
bluff. Near by is *Nanjemoy*, a post-offce of Charles
county, Maryland. Two and a quarter miles below
Smith's is *Lower Thom's Point*, a densely wooded bluff,
with yellow, sandy slopes; and opposite to this on the
right bank the mouth of Potomac Creek, which is a little
over three miles below Aquia Creek. This entrance,
which is three-fourths of a mile wide, is easily recognized
by the densely wooded bluff on its south side, which
shows two high, precipitous, sandy faces, when seen from

up river ; while the point on the north side, called *Marl-borough Point*, is low, with sandy faces fringed with trees, and has several houses on it.   The entrance to the creek presents a beautiful appearance in summer, but it is shoal, having only six feet at low tide.   The river is now making the *great bend* towards *Maryland Point*, beginning to turn to the eastward at Thom's Point on the left, and *Marlborough Point* on the right bank, running first southeast by south, and then gradually turning to east-southeast until *Maryland Point* is reached ; when it takes an east-northeast course to abreast of *Matthias Point*, nearly ten miles below.   Thus between Quantico and Matthias Point, a 'stance of about twenty-four miles, the river has describ~d an arc of nearly two-thirds of a circle.

AQUIA CREEK (SEE P. 36).

Maryland Point, commonly, though erroneously, considered the half-way point between Washington and Point Lookout, is on the north bank about two and one-half miles below *Lower Thom's Point*, and between forty-four and forty-five miles from Washington.   It is noticeable as extending out a long, low, flat arm into the river, dotted with low cedars, and having one bushy-looking cedar on its very end.   A noteworthy feature on this side of the point is a group of houses standing in a thick clump of deciduous trees ; and a number of houses on the bank close to the water, known as *Riverside*, a post village of Charles county, Md.   This is a famous *fishing-station*, and there is also a station on the south bank nearly opposite this.   The course of the river is now northeast by east, to abreast of *Matomkin Point*, about three and a half miles, and then east by north-one-half-north to *Matthias Point*, about six miles. *Matomkin Point*, eight miles below Potomac Creek, is low, and covered with bushy trees.   On the end of the point is the steamboat landing, marked by a wharf and small warehouse.   Here the south bank makes a long, gentle sweep to the southward, and then around by north-east to

Matthias Point. (See p. 39).—In this bight is the small creek known as *Jotank Creek*, noticeable for the low, heavily-wooded cliffs of reddish sand near it. Directly opposite to it on the left bank the wide entrance opening to the northward is the mouth of *Nanjemoy Creek*, three-fourths of a mile wide, and five and a half miles below Maryland Point.   It has eight feet at low tide in a narrow channel—and the shores in its vicinity are nearly all farming lands, cleared and cultivated, but diversified here and there with woods and groves of ornamental trees.   Exactly one mile below the mouth of the creek is

Upper Cedar Point, easily recognizable by the tower of the now disused lighthouse, which will appear standing in the water about half a mile from the Point.   A bell is rung in this tower in thick weather.   The point at its extremity is bluff, and covered with a dense growth of scrubby, black cedar, but the bank in its immediate vicinity, and in fact nearly as far as *Windmill Point*, at the entrance to Port Tobacco, is low and gently undulating, showing in some parts sandy faces, and in others sloping gently to the water.   It is all under cultivation. A noticeable feature in this part of the river is the high, perpendicular bluffs on the right bank between *Jotank Creek* and *Matthias Point*.   They are of reddish and yellowish sand, with tufts of scrub clinging to their faces, and a few trees on the summits. *Matthias Point*, at which is a post hamlet of King George county, Va., when seen will show as a steep, yellow bluff, dotted with scrub, with a nearly level summit, crowned with low trees.   At its base will appear the usual wharf and warehouse which mark the regular steamboat landing ; but this is not at the point itself, but just this side of it.   A quarter of a mile from the point, in a due north direction we see the *screw-pile lighthouse* which marks the last great turn in the river, which now runs nearly straight

in a southeasterly direction to the bay. We are now
nearly fifty-five and three-fourths miles from Washington,
and have opened the *Lower Cedar Point reach*, extending south by east, while to the northward, or on our left
hand the river spreads away into a broad bay, into which
empties a wide stream known as *Port Tobacco River*, and
which leads up to the settlement or village of

Port Tobacco, a post village of Charles county, Md.,
five miles above its mouth, and two miles east of the
Baltimore and Potomac railroad. It is the centre of a
fine agricultural country, and its products, as the name
implies, are to a great extent tobacco of a very fine quality. Vessels can take only two feet at low tide up to the
landing at Warehouse Point, so that only very small vessels can go up. This great estuary is all shoal—the
river channel keeping close around *Matthias Point*. The

MATTHIAS POINT (SEE P. 38).

banks ahead, which are on the east side of the *Lower
Cedar Point* reach, appear as high, precipitous sand-bluffs
fringed with trees, and with scrub clinging to the cliffs.
The sand is of a whitish color, unlike the yellow and red
sand below.

Opposite to *Matthias Point*, on the left bank as we turn
to go southward towards *Lower Cedar Point*, we will see

Pope's Creek Landing, a post village in Charles county,
Md., the mouth of the creek showing steep bluffs of reddish sand, with patches of scrub clinging to them. As
you pass the mouth of the creek, and can see into it, you
find grassy land, with low, sandy cliffs, cut up by small

ravines. The wharf at the landing marks the regular landing-place for the steamers, and there is usually a line of freight cars on the railroad track close to the bank. Pope's Creek is the terminus of that branch of the *Baltimore and Potomac* railroad.

Nearly opposite to, but a little below Pope's Creek, is *Persimmon Point*, on the right bank, low and sandy, and has a group of black-looking cedars on its end. The large *beacon* in mid-river off this point, is on a dangerous shoal with only two feet of water.

On the east bank, about two and a half miles below Pope's Creek is *Ludlow's Ferry*, and one and a half miles below this *Lower Cedar Point*, with a tall *beacon* off it in mid-river, and a *screw-pile lighthouse* to the right of the beacon. The point shows sandy faces about twenty feet high, but extends off to a long, low, flat, white point, covered with scrub and bushes. Here is

Hollister's, Westmoreland county. A large wharf and white warehouse extends into the river, and just back of the point a large white house stands in a grove of elms. This is the hotel, for this has become quite a summer resort. It is all shoal between the beacon and the point—the channel passing between the beacon and the lighthouse. The former is nearly one mile from Cedar Point; the lighthouse is on the eastern edge of the flats making off from the right bank, and is a little over a mile from shore. The channel between is quite deep, having from fifty to one hundred feet in it.

A little over three and a half miles below *Persimmon Point*, on the west bank, opens *Upper Machodoc Creek*, half a mile wide, but of no especial interest; and nearly three miles below this is *King George's Point*, low, flat, and cleared, having a couple of houses on it. It is the northern point of entrance to a small creek called Rosier's Creek. Its southern point is Bluff Point. On the left bank, four and a half miles from Lower Cedar Point is *Swan Point*, low and level, and having a large dwelling on it, surrounded by plantation huts. Between this point and Lower Cedar Point, there are two creeks—that to the northward called *Piccowaxton*, and that nearest to Swan Point, called *Cuckold's Creek;* neither of importance.

The course of the reach below Cedar Point is nearly southeast, to abreast of *Blakistone's Island*, about seventeen miles below. This is one of the most interesting parts of the river, for on it are situated three of the most noteworthy features of the trip—WASHINGTON'S BIRTH-PLACE, the NOMINI CLIFFS, and BLAKISTONE'S IS-LAND. Between *Lower Cedar Point* and the mouth of the *Wicomico River*, we cross the dangerous

Kettle-bottom Shoals, so called from their round shape on the bottom. These consist of a great number of shoal spots, occupying the whole width of the channel, and extending from *Lower Cedar Point* down the river for nearly twelve miles. The deep water channel which crosses them is marked by a line of buoys painted black and white, and placed from a mile to a mile and a half apart. We are not fairly past these shoals until we are due south from the mouth of the *Wicomico*.

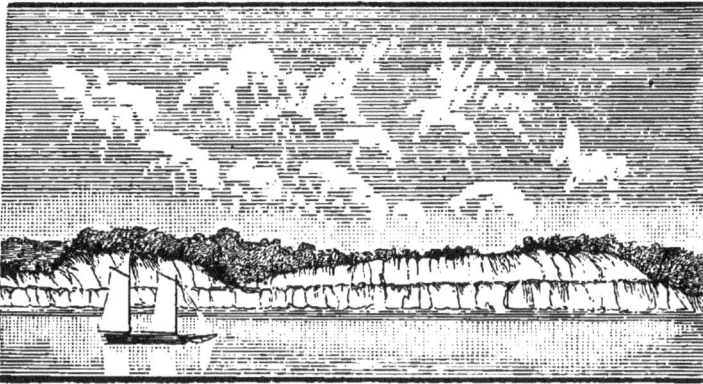

NOMINI CLIFFS (SEE P. 45).

The *mouth of this river* is between six and seven miles below Swan Point, and opens between *St. Catherine's Island* on the east, and *Cob Point* on the west. Another small island, five-eighths of a mile northwest from St. Catharine's, is called *St. Margaret's*, and contracts the entrance to one and a half miles between banks. *Wicomico* has a general northerly direction for eight miles, through a beautifully cultivated and settled country. It then divides—the main stream going to the northwestward, and a smaller stream, called *Chaptico*, turning nearly west-northwest, but both are shoal above the divide. The main channel of the river, though narrow, is deep—not less than four fathoms being found for five miles above its mouth. Beyond this it is full of shoals. The entrance is easily recognized when seen from the

river, as it looks like an island, owing to a cleared space
in the middle, which separates the woods into two groves.
On the east bank, *St. Catharine's Island* is low and flat,
but has a growth of scrubby cedars on its southwestern
end, and one very conspicuous tree on its southern face.
St. Margaret's is low, flat, entirely bare of trees except
at its southeastern end, where there is a group of small
houses, surrounded by orchards and ornamental trees.

On the right bank of the Potomac the shore curves
outward from *Bluff Point*, past *White Point*, and then
turns to the southward to *Gum Bar Point*, and thence to
Paine's Point, the western point of entrance to

Mattox Creek. This entrance is four and a half miles
below Bluff Point, and the river is here five and three-
fourths miles wide. The eastern point of entrance is
Church Point, the northwestern extremity of what was
formerly the old WASHINGTON ESTATE ; and now called
HAYWOOD. The most remarkable feature here is the
perpendicular sand-cliff which extends in an almost un-
broken line to

Pope's Creek, two and three-fourths miles below, and is
extremely level on top, and traversed about midway of its
height by a stratum of a different color, running parallel
to the line of the summit. There is so little beach at the
base that at high water there is not room to land. In a
little hollow just to the eastward of *Church Point* is seen
a fine, large weeping willow, and to the eastward of this
the chimneys and part of the roof of an ancient mansion
appear over the bluff. This is *Haywood*, once the home
of Charles Washington, but now deserted and falling into
ruin. It will well repay a visit, however. Five-eighths
of a mile below *Haywood*, makes in a very small stream
(impassable except for canoes), which is called

Bridge Creek, and from which a road leads directly to
the site of the *house where George Washington was born,*
February 22, 1732. This is about one and one-half miles
back by the road ; and the ancient *vault* is passed on the
right of the path, about five hundred yards from the
bluff. The site, represented in 1881, only by the *ruins*
of the brick chimney of the honored domicile, is on
the west bank of Pope's Creek, about three-fourths of a
mile above its mouth, and may be reached by boat
through that creek, or by *Mattox Creek* to *Wirt's Wharf,*
and thence by carriage or wagon to the *birthplace.* The

dis   e mouth of the creek to Wirt's wharf is
on(urths miles, and thence by the road it
is 1   es. The landing at *Bridge Creek* and by
boa   reek afford the best means of reaching
the   trance to this creek is seventy-two and
a h... miles from Washington.

Congress on June 17, 1879, having appropriated $3,000 for a *monument* to mark the birthplace of George Washington, and having directed the Secretary of State to carry this patriotic purpose into effect, on November 1 of the same year, Mr. Evarts, with a small party of invited guests, of which the writer was one, on the United States steamer *Tallapoosa*, visited this sacred spot. At 1 p. m., after a six hours' voyage, the steamer dropped anchor one and a half miles from Church Point. The water being shallow, the party landed in small boats. Secretary Evarts in command of the gig, General Sher-

WASHINGTON'S BIRTHPLACE IN 1881 (SEE P. 44).

man at the helm of the yawl, and Assistant Secretary Seward in charge of the whale boat. Owing to the surf, Dr. Wirt and John E. Wilson, in the carriages waiting on shore, drove into the water a distance of one hundred yards alongside of the ship's boats, and first taking the ladies, returned for the gentlemen, and landed all high and dry. Robert and Lloyd Washington welcomed the distinguished party as they landed, and all drove to the *site* of the birthplace, between Mattox and Pope creeks. C. C. Perkins, of Boston, an art connoisseur and author, one of the party; made sketches of the distinguishing objects of the place, consisting of an ancient brick chimney, a pile of bricks, a clump of fig trees, and a juniper. Thence the party visited *Wakefield*, the estate on which the birthplace is situated, then owned by John E. Wilson, and were received by his wife, Mrs. Bettie Wilson, and Mrs. Sallie Washington, her mother. This matronly dame, born 1799, was granddaughter of Augustine Washington, half-brother of George Washington, and widow of her cousin, Lawrence Washington. After partaking of lunch, the party visited the old family *cemetery*, which stood near the roadside on the way to the landing. The old vault had fallen in, and was overgrown with wild vines ; the cattle of the neighboring fields here sought the shade of the overhanging trees. After digging away the rubbish, two time-worn slabs were revealed, one bearing the name *Mildred Washington*, 1696, and the other *Jane Washington*, died 1729 : the latter was first wife to George Washington's father. Driving back to the shore in the dim light of the moon, the party in carriages were conveyed through the rolling surf to the ship's boats. All safely aboard, after a hard pull against wind and tide and splashing waves, each one clambered up the side of the steamer, and the *Tallapoosa* was soon under way back to the city.

Congress by joint resolution approved February 26, 1881, so amended and re-enacted *joint resolution* June 14, 1879, as to appropriate $30,000 to erect a monument at the birth-place of George Washington, and required, before expending the same, that the Secretary of State should be satisfied with the title to the land to be so occupied, and the securement of a public right of way thereto. Conditional deeds were given by former and later proprietors of Wakefield to the state of Virginia for parcels of land *surrounding* the vault and birthplace, and also *right of way*. Suitable accommodations to facilitate the landing of visitors are also proposed.

The *first of the Washingtons* in America, John and Laurence, sons of Sir Laurence Washington, of Sulgrave, near Malmsbury, England, emigrated to this country about 1657, and settled at Bridges creek, on the Potomac, in Westmoreland county. This Laurence Washington married Mildred Warner, of Gloucester county, and had three children, John, Augustine, and Mildred. Augustine first married Jane Butler, mentioned above as buried at Wakefield, 1729, and had three sons and a daughter. By his second wife, Mary Ball, daughter of Col. Ball, of Lancaster, married 1730, he had six children, the oldest being George, born February 22 (11 old style), 1732, on Pope's Creek, three-fourths of a mile from its junction with the Potomac. George Washington was great-grandson of the first emigrant to America, and sixth from the first Laurence of Sulgrave. The parents, soon after the birth of George, removed to Stafford county, on the Rappahannock, opposite Fredericksburg, where the father, who had a large estate, died April 12, 1743. The house in which Washington was born was destroyed by fire, which led to the removal of the family.

In June, 1815, G. W. Parke Custis placed a *slab* of freestone on the site occupied by the house, with the inscription—"HERE, THE 11 OF FEBRUARY, O. S., 1732, GEORGE WASHINGTON WAS BORN." The slab was set upon a base made of the bricks which formerly formed the hearth around which Washington in his infancy played. This stone had disappeared at the time of the writer's visit in 1879. The country which the voyager sees on the shores of the broad river, was the scene of Washington's childhood, youth, and manhood ; and here in Westmoreland, on the banks of the Rappahannock, he received the experiences which fitted him for the grave responsibilities and glory of his subsequent career.

The mother of Washington died of cancer at Fredericksburg, 1789, after his election to the Presidency of the United States. He had an affecting parting before he proceeded to the seat of Government.

Westmoreland county, defined in 1653, and commonly known as the *"Northern Neck,"* gave birth to some of the most distinguished sons of Virginia, whose names stand foremost on the roll of patriots and heroes of the struggle for national independence. Amongst them were George Washington, the two Lees, signers of the Declaration of Independence, also Thomas Francis and Arthur Lee, brothers of the famous Richard Henry Lee, the owner of *Chantilly*, on the Potomac near Pope's Creek, and once one of the finest estates of Virginia, now in ruins ; General Henry Lee, Judge Bushrod Wash-

ington, and James Monroe, President of the United States. *Stratford*, near
the Potomac just above Chantilly, was the home of Thomas Lee, father of
Richard Henry Lee, and President of the King's Council and acting Governor of Virginia. In 1879 it was still standing. His residence being burned
while governor, Stratford was erected by the government or London mer-
chants, at a cost of $80,000. It was of imported brick, contained one hun-
dred rooms, and stables for one hundred horses. The walls were two and a
half feet thick. The county, owing to the renown of its sons, was known as
The Athens of Virginia. The year Washington was born, the population of
the Neck was 3,000 souls, besides 1,000 troops for defence against the Indians.
The county has numerous water-courses and bays, abounding in fish, oysters,
and aquatic and land fowl of the finest quality. The country, too, is beautifully diversified with picturesque hills, on whose summits are ancient man-
sions, commanding a fine range of vision, taking in at a single sweep the tur-
bid flood of the Potomac in one direction, and the waters of the Rappahannock in the other.

When abreast of *Mattox Creek* coming down the river,

WASHINGTON'S BIRTHPLACE IN 1732 (SEE P. 44).

Nomini Cliffs (See page 41) will be seen on the right
or south bank, extending from about two miles below
Pope's Creek for over five miles. They appear as exceedingly steep sand-cliffs, in some cases precipitous, and
bare except for a scanty scrub growth clinging to the
faces, and cut up here and there by narrow ravines. The
summits are generally wooded, and the edge of the shore
fringed with trees. Where the cliffs are bare the color is
reddish, and they are visible for a long distance. Nearly
opposite to their eastern end on the north-bank of the
river is

Blakistone Island (See page 47).—From above it looks
like a long, low island, with clumps of low trees on its
ends, but grassy in the middle, with a large house on its
south end, surmounted by a light-tower. This is a great
summer resort, and is famous for its line-fishing (see *gen-*

eral information for fishing). It is about 79 miles below Washington. Opposite *Blakistone Island,* on the mainland, is *Coltons,* a post hamlet of St. Mary's county, Md.

On passing to the eastward of Blakistone Island, two large streams open on the north bank of the river, close together, but separated by a neck of land, with a grove of very tall elms upon it. Of these streams the westernmost is

St. Clement's Bay, one mile wide at its mouth, and six miles long, which runs in a north direction. *St. Clement's Bay,* named 1634 by Leonard Calvert, brother to Lord Baltimore, proprietor of Maryland, was the first point taken possession of under the Royal charter.

Leonard Calvert, brother of Cecil Calvert, Lord Baltimore, and first Governor of Maryland, in February, 1634, arrived at Point Comfort, Va., with about two hundred Roman Catholic settlers. In March he sailed up the Potomac, and anchoring near an island which he named St. Clement, *raised the cross, fired a cannon,* and *took possession " in the name of the Saviour of the world and the King of Great Britain,"* under the charter granted 1632. This charter was granted to Sir George Calvert, first Lord Baltimore, by King Charles First, but was executed to the son Cecil, the father having died two months before. It granted the present state of Maryland, though within the charter of Virginia. The territory was actually in occupation by Virginia at Kent Island, opposite the future site of Annapolis.

The other is *Breton Bay,* one mile wide at its mouth, and five and a half miles long, which runs in an easterly and then northeasterly direction to the interesting little post village of *Leonardstown.* county-seat of St. Mary's county, Md., and named after Leonard Calvert, who arrived in this vicinity in 1634, at the head of the first settlers of Maryland. The Southern Maryland railroad passes within two miles. You may carry not less than nine feet in St. Clement's up to the head of the bay, but it is not much used. The same can be carried up to *Leonardtown* in Breton bay, through a crooked channel. The country is cultivated and rich, and in summer is very beautiful.

On the south bank of the river, the wide and deep bight that makes in about two miles to the eastward of the lower end of Nomini Cliffs is

Nomini Bay, which receives the waters of Nomini creek. Its eastern point is called *Kingcopsico Point,* and is remarkable only for the thick growth of cedar trees on its very end. It is quite low and flat. On the Nomini Bay, Patrick Spence and —— Monroe, one of the President's ancestors, had a warehouse before 1732. Two miles below is the mouth of the *Lower Machodoc* river, one and one-fourth miles wide at its mouth. It has good water in it. This vicinity is a great place for oysters. One and three-fourth miles below the mouth of the Machodoc is *Ragged Point*, low and wooded, except at its extremity, which is a mere bare sand spit.

On the north shore, as soon as we pass *Blakistone Island*, we see to the northward, about one and one-half miles off, and one mile east of Blakistone's, a little islet about five hundred yards long, composed merely of sand. It is called HERON ISLAND, and divides the channels leading into *Breton and St. Clement's bays*. It is surrounded by dangerous shoals, which, however feared by navigators, are the source of revenue to the fishermen during the season ; as it is on the edge of these flats that

BLAKISTONE ISLAND (SEE P. 4).

the fish come to feed. The river is nearly five and one-half miles wide between Kingkopsico Point and the mouth of Breton Bay.

When abreast of *Ragged Point*, we perceive nearly ahead, and about five miles off on the north bank of the river, a low, squat, white light-tower, and a dwelling-house with a red roof. This is *Piney Point Lighthouse*, on

Piney Point, which is low, flat, and grassy. As we approach, a dazzling white fence is seen around the light-tower and dwelling, and soon other white houses are seen among the thick trees. On coming abreast of this point, we see a level beach backed by grassy land covered with low, bushy trees, among which are several long, low, white houses in a line a short distance back. This is the site of the summer watering place, and the houses are the hotel and its adjoining cottages and outbuildings. A tall flag-staff is seen among the trees, and there is a very good wharf for the steamboats which go and come daily during the season. This place is much frequented during the summer, on account of the bathing and fishing. Piney Point is also a post village of St. Mary's county, Md. The river is here only three and three-fourths miles wide, but has a deep channel ninety feet deep, about one mile southwest of the lighthouse. At

PINEY POINT.

Ragged Point, on the right bank of the Potomac turns abruptly, and runs nearly south by east, two and a half miles to *Jackson's Creek*, and then about south-east for six miles to *Lynch's Point*, the northern point of entrance to *Wicomico River*.

St. George's Island.—This island is two and a half miles long, low, and nearly level, and diversified with cleared lands and groves of trees. A narrow inlet separates its northern end from Piney Point beach, and this opening communicates with *St. George's Creek*, affording fine facilities for smooth-water sailing, rowing, and fishing. *St. George's Creek* separates the island from the mainland on the northeast. When abreast of the southeastern end of the island we open the historical •

St. Mary's River, on which was made the earliest settlement in the state of Maryland. The *St. Mary's River* is two and one-half miles wide at its mouth, and runs nearly north, with not less than twenty-one feet at low tide as far up as the village of St. Mary's, six miles above. It then turns northwesterly for three and a half

miles to its head. The shores are very beautiful in summer, and it would repay an excursionist to visit *Priest's
Point*, the site of the ancient church (now destroyed),
and the little post village of *St. Mary's*, both of which
are on the east bank, and are easily accessible. The
eastern point of the river is called *Kitt's Point*, low and
cleared, and three and a half miles above is *Priest's
Point*, easily distinguishable by the large frame house
with many windows, which is the dormitory and refectory
for the theological students at this place. On approach-
ing the point it is seen to be level, with perpendicular,
sandy faces, and on the extremity is a wind-mill. Behind
the mill, and a little farther back from shore, are the ruins
of two large brick houses, formerly occupied as a church

PRIEST'S POINT AND SEMINARY.

and priest's house. The large wooden building near the
beach is occupied as a sort of summer resort for rest and
recreation for the students for the priesthood, but there
are also several Roman Catholic clergymen here in charge.
There is good bathing abreast of the house. The clergy-
man in charge is courteous, and will show the site of the
ancient church if desired. Two miles and a half above
Priest's Point is the village of *St. Mary's*, on the east
bank, and opposite to it on the west bank is *West St.
Mary's*. Both are quite small hamlets, only of importance on account of their age.

Leonard Baltimore, from *St. Clement Island*, (for which see, page 46) sailed
up the Potomac River to Piscataway Creek, where Fort Washington now
stands, and but twelve miles from the present city of Washington. Here he
opened negotiations with the chief of the Indian village on shore, but finally
determined for greater security to settle nearer the bay, and after exploring
the shore, purchased an Indian village, which then stood on the site of the present St. Mary's, and founded a settlement April, 1634. The charter, which was

framed by Lord Baltimore himself, and a Roman Catholic, was constructed on principles of religious toleration. In 1635, the first Legislative Assembly convened at St. Mary's, and a representative government of the people was formally established in 1639. Religious troubles soon broke out, and were a source of much disorder between Catholics and Protestants, and during the religious wars in England ; but the colony thrived, and with a slight interruption as a royal province, it remained under the proprietaries until it became an independent state of the American Confederation.

The Potomac attains its greatest width between the *St. Mary's* and the *Coan* rivers, being nearly seven miles wide. The line joining *Point Lookout and Smith's Point* at the mouth (which is eleven and a half miles) not being at right angles to the course of the river, is therefore not a fair measure of its width. The true width at Point Lookout is six and a half miles. On the right bank, three and a half miles to the eastward of Wicomico river, is the mouth of

Coan River, also famous for its oysters, and we may add for its oyster-roasts. It is a mile and a half wide at its mouth, but rapidly contracts, and gives off two branches to the eastward—*Kingscote Creek* and *The Glebe*. There is good water in this river and its branches ; but the channel is narrow and crooked. In shad season this is a famous place for *planked shad parties*. parties.

From here the south shore of the river runs nearly southeast by east for thirteen and a half miles to

Smith's Point, the south point of entrance to the river —but by vessels bound up the bay little of this shore is seen, as the course turns to the northward, passing close to *Point Lookout*. The south shore will therefore appear simply as a long line of dark woods to Smith's Point— which will be more particularly mentioned in the excursion to Norfolk. On the north bank of the river below the St. Mary's there is nothing of interest except

Point Lookout. The shore is cut up by little creeks, such as *Smith's Creek, Calvert's Creek, Harry James Creek*, etc., and is all low, level, and cultivated.

For SMITH'S POINT see EXCURSION III, From the Mouth of the Potomac to Norfolk.

For POINT LOOKOUT see EXCURSION VI, From the Mouth of the Potomac to Baltimore.

EXCURSION III.

From Washington to Fortress Monroe and Norfolk, Va.

DISTANCE FROM WASHINGTON

To SMITH'S POINT (Mouth Potomac) . . 119 Miles.
To FORTRESS MONROE . . . . . . 183 "
To NORFOLK . . . . 194 "

TABLE OF DISTANCES

From the *Mouth of the Potomac* (Smith's Point) to points
on the Chesapeake Bay, compiled by the United
States Coast and Geodetic Survey.

FROM SMITH'S POINT (MOUTH OF POTOMAC) TO

	Miles.		Miles.
Wicomico River	6	York River Spit Lighthouse .	49
Windmill Point	18½	Back River Lighthouse . . .	57¼
Rappahannock River Spit . .	21	Old Point Comfort (Fortress	
Stingray Point	21½	Monroe	64
Wolf Trap Spit	30½	Newport News Point	71
New Point Comfort . . .	39	Norfolk	75

[**Note.**—Returning over this route, the reader will follow the narrative in
the reverse order.]

The points of interest in the voyage from WASHING-
TON TO THE MOUTH OF THE POTOMAC, will be found
fully described in EXCURSION II.

If we are bound to *Old Point Comfort (Fortress Monroe)* or *Norfolk* from *Washington*, we turn to the southward when we reach the mouth of the Potomac, and pass
close to an iron, screw-pile *light-house*, eighty-five feet
high, standing about two and one-fourth miles from shore.
This is *Smith's Point lighthouse*, and is placed on the end
of the long shoal making out from that known as
Smith's Point, the south point of the *entrance to the
Potomac*, and appears when seen from the eastward as a
low, flat surface, covered with scrubby trees, and having

(51)

a tall, white light-tower on a white, sandy beach on its eastern end. A long, low point of dense black woods juts out to the westward of the light-tower, marking the entrance to the *Little Wicomico River.* Smith's Point is also a post hamlet of Northumberland county, Virginia. We have now entered the *Chesapeake Bay.*

THE CHESAPEAKE BAY.

The *Chesapeake Bay,* the largest inland water of the kind in the United States, extends from the mouth of the Susquehanna river, about latitude 39° 37' north, to Old Point Comfort, about latitude 37° north, a *distance* of about two hundred miles, and has a *width* varying from four to ten miles in the upper, and twenty to forty miles in the lower bay. Its *outlet* into the Atlantic Ocean is between *Cape Charles* on the north, and *Cape Henry* on the south, both in Virginia. The *distance* from cape to cape is fifteen miles. From the head of the bay to latitude 38° north, its waters are entirely in Maryland, and south of that parallel in Virginia. The *eastern shore,* a peninsula with the Atlantic on the east and bay on the west, embraces eight counties in Maryland and two in Virginia. The bay, from the capes almost to the mouth of the Susquehanna has a depth sufficient for vessels of the greatest draught. It is also indented with a great number of *inlets* and *estuaries,* through some of which empty the important *rivers,* such as the Susquehanna, Elk, Choptank, Patuxent, Nanticoke, and Potomac, in Maryland, and the Rappahannock, York, and James, in Virginia, and innumerable rivers of less importance. The Patapsco, upon which is Baltimore, and the Severn, upon which stands Annapolis, are really parts of the bay.

The Chesapeake Bay also abounds in fish of great variety and of the finest quality, and the innumerable bights are filled with an abundance of game which resorts to salt and fresh water.

On the Atlantic coast south of Cape Henry, the sounds, estuaries, and rivers are shallow, and offer but few good harbors. Following the coast northward, the Chesapeake is the first of a series of deep and commodious bays from Virginia to Maine.

Nearly six miles to the southward of *Smith's Point* is

the entrance to the *Great Wicomico River*, two miles wide at its mouth. The *eastern shore* of the bay being all low marsh, is scarcely visible, and not at all noticeable to parties passing down the main channel. The main entrance to

Tangier Sound, famous for oysters, is opposite to the Great Wicomico, but the bay is here nearly fifteen miles wide, so only the western shore is seen. Many small inlets penetrate this western shore.

The *greatest width* of the bay is reached at *Dimer's Creek*, fifteen and a half miles below Smith's Point, and four miles above *Windmill Point*, the north point of entrance to the *Rappahannock*. Here the width, with an almost unobstructed channel, is very nearly twenty-five miles from shore to shore! *Windmill Point*, the north point of entrance to th

SMITH'S POINT (SEE P. 51.)

Rappahannock, is eighteen and one-half miles below the mouth of the Potomac. *Rappahannock Spit* makes off from this point in a southeast direction, and a screw-pile light-house, placed on its end, about two and three-eighths miles off shore, serves to mark the entrance. The river is nearly three and three fourths miles wide, and its southern point, called *Stingray Point*, is also marked by a screw-pile light-house, built in the water one and three-eighths miles from the point. At night a red light is shown from this light-house, while that on the north side, on Rappahannock Spit, is white.

In April, 1813, a flotilla of 12 armed gun-boats, from Cockburn's fleet, entered the mouth of the Rappahanock, and made an attack on the Dolphin, a Baltimore privateer, 10 guns, and three schooners about to sail for France. A desperate contest followed, and the schooners were soon disposed of; but the Dolphin was only taken, after a desperate encounter on her decks, against the overwhelming numbers of the British.

Stingray Point also forms the northern point of entrance to the

Piankatank River, a deep but crooked stream, penetrating this shore about twelve miles. It is famous for its oysters. *Hill's Bay,* on its southern bank, being especially noted. The river is nearly three miles wide at its mouth, but rapidly contracts, and at *Iron Point,* less than four miles inside its mouth, it is but seven-eighths of a mile wide. This river is ninety-seven miles long to Fredericksburg, at the head of navigation.

Wolf Trap Spit, a long shoal making out from the west shore is a little over nine miles below the *Rappahannock,* and has on its eastern extremity a screw-pile light-house, two and seven-eighths miles from the nearest land. This light-house shows at night a fixed white light, varied by bright flashes to distinguish it from its neighbors. Nearly nine miles below it we will see the white tower on *New Point Comfort,* at the north point of entrance to *Mobjack Bay,* and directly opposite to *Cherrystone Inlet,* on the east shore. Here the bay is scarcely fourteen miles wide, and the

Eastern Shore is just visible from the channel.

The *eastern shore* here is in Virginia, and consists of the two isolated counties of Accomac, established in 1673, and Northampton, in 1634, under the original name of Accomac Shire, and changed to its present name in 1673. This is the southern point of the Peninsula. The soil and climate are excellent, and gardening the chief pursuit. The fig and pomegranate thrive, and the castor bean is a staple. Here the old-time fashion *Virginia hospitality* and the antique gig still reign in all their ancient sway. Many ancient records are also here preserved.

Mobjack Bay is a great indentation in the western shore, which receives the waters of East, North, Ware, and Severn rivers; it is about four miles wide, and has plenty of water in it, but is only of importance on account of its oysters, which are of excellent quality. A steamboat runs here twice a week from Norfolk and Old Point. The mouth of the

York River is marked by a screw-pile light-house, built on the end of *York Spit,* over seven miles from the nearest land. At night it shows a red light. The shores on both sides of the entrance to this river are low marsh, but once inside, the land is fast and very generally cultivated. There is another screw-pile light-house of *Too's Point,* the southern point of entrance; here the river

VIEW OF FORTRESS MONROE (SEE P. 56).   (55)

is two and a half miles wide. On this river, seven miles above Too's Point is

Yorktown, the scene of the surrender, October 19, 1783, of Marquis Cornwallis and his whole army of 8,054 troops, sailors, and marines. *Congress* appropriated for the erection of a suitable *monument* on the site of the surrender, and preparations are being made, under the auspices of Congress, for a becoming celebration of the centennial anniversary of the British surrender.

The river has a length of thirty-two miles to

West Point, where it branches, the western branch being known as the *Pamunkey* river, and leading up to the *White House*, famous in the history of the army of the Potomac. The *eastern branch*, called the *Mattapony*, was also well known during the Rebellion, 1861-65.

To the southward of the *York River* we begin to approach the land on the west side, and a white light-tower will soon be seen standing on the beach. This is *Back River Light-house*, which shows a fixed white light, flashing brightly at intervals of one and a half minutes ; and the opening is the mouth of *Back River*. The light is the first indication of the approach to '

Old Point Comfort, being only about six and one-fourth miles to the northward of it. The light-house on the latter point will be visible from abreast of *Back River Light*, and also the lines of *Fortress Monroe*, the huge barracks-like buildings of the *Hygeia Hotel*, and the tall dome of the *Soldier's Home* at Hampton. The *hotel is* noticeable for its tall mansard cupola, and, on a nearer approach, for the large pavillion with striped roof in front of it.

Old Point Comfort (Fortress Monroe) is eleven miles from Norfolk. The *Fortress* stands on the point at the entrance to *Hampton Roads*, and the *Rip Raps* are opposite at a distance of 1900 yards. The *Fortress* affords a safe *anchorage* in time of war, and guards the *approach* to Hampton Roads, the Chesapeake Bay, and the James River A *fort* stood here in 1812.

Fortress Monroe is a granite, casemated work, surmounted by traverses and parapet of earth, (see p. 55.) A large water-battery of granite, also casemated, stands on the beach in front of the southeastern angle of the works. There is quite a settlement at Old Point on the government grounds ; and it is a great summer-resort, the travel thither increasing every year. You can reach

Hampton either by hiring a carriage, which can always be obtained in front of the hotel, or by steamer.

The village is on *Hampton Creek*, about two and a half miles from the wharf at Old Point, and fourteen miles from Norfolk. The points of interest are the Hampton Academy for colored and Indian youth, and the Soldier's Home. It was also the scene of a desperate conflict in the war of 1812.

To avenge their *defeat* at *Craney Island*, the British attacked Hampton, the county seat of Elizabeth county, Va. There were 450 Virginia militia and a handful of artillerymen here to *defend* the village. On the night of June 24, 2500 British troops were *landed* in boats, under cover of a sloop of war, two miles from the town. Admiral Cockburn meantime made a *feint* off Blackbeard's Point, at the mouth of Hampton Creek. The Americans opened a brisk *fire* on the boats, and soon drove them under shelter under the point. The land troops advancing were warmly received and at first thrown into a *panic;* but, recovering, again *advanced,* and again the Americans, on Celey's road, charged and drove them back, killing a Lieutenant-Colonel and a number of men. While in pursuit, the British suddenly *opened* a storm of grape, canister, and rockets immediately in front of the attacking force of Americans, causing them to break. This turned the tide of battle. The British followed up their advantage, executing a flank movement, threatening the American line of retreat, thus ending the battle; and entered Hampton by the Yorktown road. The village was given up to pillage, and the women, old and young, to treatment which only the license of barbarous war would countenance. The atrocities, particularly on the women, caused a sense of indignation and horror even in England, and throughout the civilized world. Sir Charles Napier, in his diary, says, "Every horror was perpetrated with impunity—rape, murder, pillage—and not a man was punished." Cockburn, to stimulate his men, who were getting worsted, promised "booty and beauty."

Directly south of the light-house at *Old Point*, and in the middle of the roads is a warlike structure in the shape of a casemated work of granite, standing apparently in the water, but in an unfinished condition. This is *Fort Wool*, built upon the northern end of the shoal of *Willoughby's Point*, called the

Rip-Raps.—It was intended for harbor defence. At the beginning of the Rebellion, a twenty-inch Rodman gun, throwing a 1,250 pound projectile, was mounted here. The completion of the fort was practically abandoned after the late war.

The *Rip Raps*, originally the shoal water which, under the action of the waves on a bar was kept in a constant ripple, received this name, comprised an area of five acres, the greatest part twenty-two feet below the surface of the water, and the rest eighteen feet. On this space an island was raised by throwing rocks in the water, and a castle of defense was commenced. This was carried up to the first embrasure, but, owing to the settling of the foundation, it was abandoned. It now remains unfinished; but, like a sentinel, stands to guard the doorway to the "American Mediterranean."

The great area of water extending from Old Point Comfort to the mouth of the James river is known as

Hampton Roads, the estuary of the James river, which affords one of the most commodious, though not always comfortable, and finest anchorages in the world, and has a depth sufficient for the largest vessels. It is about six miles long east and west, by four miles north and south, and has water sufficient for the largest vessels. The *James River* flows into its western end, the *Nansemond* into its southwestern, and the *Elizabeth* into its southeastern side. As we come into the roads, a remarkable looking, white, sandy point, like a low bluff, will be seen to the southward, apparently marking the southern limits of the anchorage. It is crowned with low, black-looking trees. This is *Sewall's Point*, the eastern point of entrance to the *Elizabeth River*, and celebrated during the war as the site of effective *batteries*. To the westward the low, sandy point, covered with a scanty growth of scrub, with here and there a lone, tall tree, and showing a few houses on the beach, is *Newport News Point*, the northern point of entrance to James river. Between these two points—*Sewall's* and *Newport News*—took place some of the most exciting events of the late war.

Here the *Merrimac*, coming down the Elizabeth from Norfolk, encountered and destroyed the frigates *Cumberland and Congress;* and here she herself was defeated and driven back to Norfolk by the *Monitor*, under command of Commodore Worden. Here rendezvoused the *great fleets* that went forth to attack Port Royal in 1861 and Fort Fisher in 1864. It was off Newport News Point that the plucky Davidson, formerly a lieutenant in our navy, brought down the torpedo boat "*Snipe*" in the middle of the night, and placed and exploded a huge torpedo under the bottom of the frigate *Minnesota*, the flag ship of the North Atlantic squadron. Fortunately, the torpedo exploded exactly under the shot-room, and the heavy solid shot formed a mass too powerful for the explosion to overcome. The ship was not seriously injured, though her people were badly scared. Davidson escaped with his little craft, and arrived safely at Richmond. It was off Newport News also that the cruiser *Florida* was "accidentally" sunk when it was found that international law would probably compel the United States to return her to Brazil, and to the port of Bahia, whence she was cut out. She was sent up to Newport News by Admiral Porter, and anchored in nine fathoms. Shortly after, a powerful steamer belonging to the Quartermaster's department of the army of the James, ran into her at night, and sunk her. Her officers and crew were saved. In the *Nansemond* took place some of the severest naval fighting of the war. Lieutenant Lamson and Lieutenant Cushing, in two small purchased gun boats, harrassed the enemy to such an extent that they were finally obliged to entirely withdraw from the river banks. Both officers received the thanks of the department for their services.

Leaving Fortress Monroe, we proceed directly over towards *Sewall's Point*, bound up to *Norfolk*.

Craney Island *Lighthouse*, a little over one-half a mile to the northeast of the island of that name, lies close in with the west shore of the river. It is easily recognized by the *earthwork* on its eastern end, and the buildings belonging to the Naval Magazine, which is established on this island.

A *British fleet*, consisting of four seventy-four gun frigates and eight vessels, carrying from twenty to forty-four guns, and a number of smaller vessels, under Admiral Sir George Cockburn, with 1800 men, and appliances for landing, arrived in Hampton roads in February , 1813. The *militia* of the country around Norfolk and the Peninsula, rallied to defence. *Fortifications* were thrown up at *Craney Island*, five miles below Norfolk, and every preparation to meet the enemy was made.

In June, 1813, Admiral Warren, with his fleet, and Sir Sidney Beckwith in command of troops and marines, *entered Hampton Roads*, and, after destroying vessels on the James, turned his attention to Norfolk. The defenses consisted of the Constellation and twenty gun boats, Forts Norfolk and Nelson on either side of the mouth of the Elizabeth River, Craney Island, containing thirty acres, and Forts Tar and Barbour on the land side.

It was determined to make the defense at Craney Island. The whole force of *Americans* on the island the night before the attack (June 21, 1813,) was 737 men, including 30 regulars, 150 seamen, and the rest volunteers and militia. The *British* landed 2500 infantry and marines at Hoffleur's Creek on the main land, and moved up to Wise's Creek and beyond, to get the American rear. Simultaneously with this movement, 50 barges, with 1500 seamen and marines, approached from the British fleet, led by Admiral Warren's beautiful *barge*, the Centipede, fifty feet long, and manned by twenty-four oarsmen, carrying a brass three-pounder, and commanded by Captain Hanchett, a natural son of George III. As the barges approached, the Americans waited until they reached within range, and then opened a terrible fire. After resisting for awhile, the British were thrown into great confusion. The Admiral's barge was hulled, wounding several of the men, including her commander, and went to the bottom ; four others also sunk, and the rest of the flotilla retreated to the ships. The result was mortifying to the British. Discomfited and routed on water and land, they abandoned any further demonstrations against Norfolk.

After the repulse of the British, June, 1813, Craney Island was fortified. A fort was erected on the southeast end of the island, and a brick magazine and breastworks on the northwestern, with a connecting line of entrenchments on the channel side of the island, with embrasures for cannon. The *embankments* are still visible.

The fort on the right bank of the Elizabeth river, with the gently sloping lawn, dotted with pyramids of shot and shell, and occupied by a red-brick house, is **Fort Norfolk**, built during the war of the Revolution, 1776–83, and was the powder depot for the navy before it was removed to Craney Island. On the south side of this point is *Paradise Creek*, shallow and unimportant ; while nearly directly opposite to the Naval Hospital wharf is *Town Point*, the northwest extremity of Norfolk. The large, square mooring buoys between this point and Fort Norfolk mark the usual *"Navy Anchorage,"* as it is called, for vessels intending to take in powder and other ammunition.

Norfolk, in Norfolk county, created in 1691, lies on the north bank of Elizabeth river, has one of the most commodious and secure *harbors*, at all seasons, in the world. It is also completely fortified. The *Navy Yard, Dry Dock, Marine Hospital*, etc., once were the finest under government. It is the great *commercial* port of Virginia, and the entrepot of the produce from the south *via* the *Dismal Swamp Canal*. Before the war of 1812 it controlled the West India trade of this region. Its *City Hall* is very fine. It is also an important *railroad centre*, and from here a line of *ocean steamers* departs for the principal northern sea-ports.

Norfolk is also the northern terminus of the *Dismal Swamp Canal*, twenty-two miles long, constructed in 1829 through the mire and aqueous vegetation of the Dismal Swamp, to connect the waters of the Chesapeake Bay in Virginia, and Albemarle and Pamlico Sounds of North Carolina. This remarkable *morass* is thirty miles long and ten miles wide, and is overgrown with an impenetrable network of reeds, bamboo, briars, cypress, cedar, and gall-bush. In winter and summer vegetation wears a perennial hue.

At *Norfolk* the river branches—the main stream keeping nearly due south past

Portsmouth and Gosport, at which latter place is situated the Navy Yard, while the Eastern Branch keeps to the eastward, skirting the wharf line on the south side of the city, and affording dock-room for nearly all of the carrying trade which comes here. The only prominent buildings seen from the river on the Norfolk side are the *Custom House*, which is of granite with pillars in front—and the Atlantic Hotel, a large brick structure.

The Navy Yard at

Gosport shows its large ship-houses and the tall masts of the receiving-ship from below *Town Point*. This naval station, which used to be the most important of all the dock-yards on the Atlantic coast, is of interest now to travelers only as having been the yard where the Merrimac was refitted and iron-plated ; and whence she went forth on her mission of destruction. Many relics of her, as well as of the old Pennsylvania, ship of the line, which was destroyed when the yard was evacuated by our forces, are preserved and shown to visitors. When the rebellion broke out, the *Navy Yard* at Gosport, with several million dollars' worth of Government property and vessels, were destroyed or seized (April, 1861) by the Confederates of Virginia.

EXCURSION IV.

From Washington via Fortress Monroe and Norfolk to Richmond.

From Washington
To Old Point Comfort (Fortress Monroe) 183 Miles.
To Norfolk . . . . 194 "
To Richmond . . . . .300 "

TABLE OF DISTANCES

From Old Point Comfort to points on the James River, compiled by the Coast and Geodetic Survey.

From Old Point Comfort to

	Miles.		Miles.
Newport News Point	7	Jamestown Island (Southeast End)	34
Pig Point (Entrance to Nansemond River)	10	Chickahominy Entrance . . .	45
White Shoal Lighthouse (Day's Point)	14½	Wilson's Wharf	50
		Windmill Point	57½
Mulberry Island	22	Harrison's Landing	63
Point of Shoals Lighthouse .	23	Jordan's Point	66
Deep Water Shoals Lighthouse .	26	City Point	69
Hog Island	29½	Dutch Gap Canal	91
Swan's Point	36	Richmond	109

The tourist, for the *voyage from Washington to the Mouth of the Potomac*, will see Excursion II., and from the mouth of the Potomac *to Norfolk*, Excursion III. At Norfolk the tourists can take one of the fine *river steamers* for Richmond. Tourists *returning* will read in reverse order.

THE JAMES RIVER.

The *Cow Pasture River*, the principal fountain-stream of the *James*, has its *source* on the slopes of the great North Mountain, in Pendleton county, Virginia, and within sight of the headwaters of the Potomac Where Jackson and Cow Pasture rivers unite in the defiles between Potts and Mill mountains, the stream first receives the name of THE JAMES.

(61)

On its winding course through the bold and picturesque succession of mountain ranges of Virginia, it traverses a romantic gap in the Blue Ridge, within sight of
the celebrated *Peaks of Otter*. From this point the
stream is navigable, and traverses some of the richest
and most beautiful counties included in the expansive
valley of the James, from Old Point Comfort to the Allegheny mountains, a distance of 225 miles, and a mean
width of 50 miles. At the *Falls at Richmond* it meets
the tide, and thence resembles a lake more than a river,
and enters the Chesapeake Bay between Willoughby
Point and Old Point Comfort, after a course of five hundred and eight miles from its headwaters. The river has
a rapid descent in places. Its source is 2,500 feet above
tide. At the Blue Ridge it is 800 feet, at Lynchburg
500 feet, and at Columbia, 175 feet.

The distance from *Old Point Comfort* to *Richmond*, by
the *James River*, is one hundred and nine miles, but its
navigation above *Harrison's Landing* is exceedingly
difficult, owing to the narrowness and crookedness of the
channel. On leaving
Old Point Comfort, the steamer heads to the westward
towards Newport News. Since the settlement of this
point as the terminus of the new branch road from Richmond, a village has grown up, as the *Point* has all the
advantages of good water and accessibility.

Newport News was named after Captain Christopher Newport, who
landed here, with Captain John Smith, from his ships, in May, 1607, while
exploring the shores prior to the selection of Jamestown Island for the proposed
settlement.

On the *south shore*, the eastern point of entrance to the
Nansemond, Pig Point, will be seen. A settlement was
established here in 1609, from Jamestown, and was destroyed by the Indians in the Indian massacre a few years
later. The western point of entrance to the James,
which is called *Fishing Point*, is low and level, but is
covered with an exceptionally heavy growth of trees.
Seen from the Newport News side it appears like a group
of islands. The insular appearance is caused by the
marsh between the fast lands, on which are the trees.
The river is here a little over three miles wide. Above
Newport News Point there are no objects of special
interest except the mouth of *Pagan Creek*, which leads
up to *Smithfield*, famous for its hams. Almost directly

opposite is the mouth of *Warwick River*. The screw-pile light-house, in mid-river nearly midway between the mouth of Pagan Creek and the east shore, is *Deep Water Shoal Light*, and we leave it close to on the starboard hand. After passing *Day's Point*, the north point of Pagan creek, the steamer enters the deep bight called *Burwell's Bay*, and comes to *Point of Shoals Light*, another screw-pile structure on the western end of the great oyster-beds off the bay, and marking the turning-point in the channel.

Both shores of the river show alternate cultivated lands and woods. Beyond *Burwell's Bay* is

Mulberry Point, the north end of *Mulberry Island* (see *Hog Island* below) which separates *Warwick River*

JAMESTOWN ISLAND (SEE P. 64).

from the James. The river now turns to the northward, and we see ahead *Deep Water Shoals Light*. The channel passes on its western side. Beyond and opposite this light is

Hog Island, to which the Jamestown settlers repaired when about to abandon the settlement.

Scarcity of provisions, bad administration, and universal disorder having caused great disappointment, at a council it was determined to return to England. On June 10, 1610, at night, all having gone aboard, the two vessels dropped down to *Hog Island*, and next morning fell down to *Mulberry Point*. Here the deserting settlers spied Lord Delaware's ships. But for his timely arrival they would have been away on the ocean. Lord Delaware induced them to return, and Jamestown Island was reoccupied, never to be again abandoned.

At *Tavern Point*, which is four and a half miles above Deep Water Shoals light, the river turns abruptly to the southwestward. The low, marshy shore on the north and west, interspersed with spurs of high pine woods, is

Jamestown Island, the site of the first permanent settlement made by the English on these shores. The ruins of the old church still remain, and are visible from the river. They stand upon *Church Point*, near the northwest end of the island, in a grove of trees; and seen from the river look more like the ruins of a brick tower than anything else. Abreast of the old church the river is only one and one-eighth miles wide, the southwest point being known as *Swan's Point*.

After the repeated failures of Raleigh at Roanoke Inlet under the patents of 1584, leaving nothing but the name Virginia, after Elizabeth the Virgin queen, in December, 1606, Captain John Smith, with three ships, was sent out by the London company, and, after a cruise through the Caribbean Islands, anchored within the mouth of the Bay of Chesapeake. Before landing, he named the south cape Henry, and the north Charles, in honor of the king's two eldest sons, and the river, which the Indians called Powhatan, he called James, after his sovereign. Smith made a careful exploration of the river for an eligible location for a settlement. Finally he chose a site thirty-four miles up the river, " which, besides the goodness of the soil, was esteemed as most fit and capable to be made a place both of trade and security, two-thirds thereof being environed by the main river, which affords good anchorage all along, and the other third by a small narrow river, capable of receiving many vessels of a hundred tons quite as high as till it meets within thirty yards of the main river again, and where, at the spring tides, it overflows into the main river."

The island contained about 2000 acres of highland, and good pasture.

Robert Beverley, in his excellent history of Virginia, printed in London, 1722, alluding to the cupidity of the first settlers, says, "They found in a neck of land on the back of Jamestown Island a fresh stream of water springing out of a small bank, which washed down a yellow sort of dust-isinglass which, being cleansed by the fresh streaming of the water, lay shining in the bottom of that limpid element, and stirred up in them an unseasonable and inordinate desire after riches. * * * They spoke not nor thought of anything but gold. * * * Accordingly, they put into this ship all the yellow dirt they had gathered, and what skins and furs they had trucked for, and sent her away." This was in 1607. Soon after, a second ship was thus loaded. From Jamestown, Smith explored the Bay and James and Potomac rivers.

James City county, in which Jamestown Island is situated, was one of the eight original shires into which the colony of Virginia was divided by the legislature of 1634.

In June, 1619, Gov. Sir George Yeardley called the *first legislative assembly* on the American continent. The representatives were elected, the counties not yet having been established, by townships, the boroughs of Jamestown, Henrico, Bermuda Hundred, and others, sending their delegates. The Lower Branch received the name of *House of Burgesses*. The acts passed by this assembly were sent to the London company to be read in the court, and to be confirmed or annulled.

In 1698, a great fire having occurred at Jamestown, consuming the public records, the capital of the colony was removed to Williamsburg, settled in 1632, seven miles from Jamestown, and remained there until removed to Richmond in 1779.

At Swan's Point the James makes another turn—the river running nearly west for over five miles to *Dancing Point*, the western point of entrance to the

Chickahominy River.—This small and ordinarily insignificant stream has a place in history from its intimate connection with the operations of the Army of the Potomac in 1862-63. The river, running in a northerly direction, is navigable for light-draught vessels for about seven miles, after which it turns to the northwestward, and passes about seven miles back of the city of Richmond. Its banks are mostly a *deadly swamp*, affording good sport to the hunter, but brought to the unacclimated army more devastation than the bullet.

A mile beyond Dancing Point is one of the famous plantations of ancient days, known as *Sandy Point*, once the home of the famous Harry Lee, known in Revolutionary times as "Light-horse Harry;" now in other hands. Directly opposite to it on the south bank of the river is *Sloop Point*, a high, steep bluff, covered with trees. Here the river is three-fourths of a mile wide, with a depth of from twenty-four to thirty feet.

THE RUINS OF JAMESTOWN (SEE P. 64).

One mile and a quarter above this point, where you will see a long wharf built out, is *Claremont*, another large plantation of old days.

On the north side of *Chipoak* begin the famous *Brandon Plantations*, called *Lower and Upper Brandon*, occupying the whole width of the peninsula between this reach and the next. The river here runs nearly due north three and three-fourths miles to *Kennon's Marsh*. At *Lower Brandon*, whose landing is about seven-eighths of a mile above *Chipoak Creek*, the large two-story brick house seen through the trees is the mansion. *Upper Brandon* joins *Lower Brandon* on the northwest, but its front is on the next reach, and is not seen until we we have rounded *Kennon's Marsh*. *Kennon's Marsh* is quite extensive, and occupies the whole of the north end of the peninsula. Directly opposite to it on the north bank is *Kennon's Plantation*, on a bare bluff about thirty feet high. The mansion and outbuildings when seen from the river form in appearance quite a settlement. Here the river is only six hundred and fifty yards wide, with a depth of from thirty to one hundred feet.

At Kennon's the river makes another sharp bend,. and runs nearly southwest for four miles, with an average width of three-fourths of a mile—to *Weynoak Point*. We pass the small plantation of *Milton*, three-fourths of a mile above Kennon's, and then we come to the landing of *Upper Brandon*, where there is a long wharf. The fields are level and cleared, and glimpses of the houses of the plantation may be obtained here and there through the trees that fringe the shore. *Dunmore Plantation* adjoins Upper Brandon on the south side, being separated from it by a small creek, with thickly-wooded banks. The shore is a sand-bluff fringed with trees, and so continues to the mouth of *Ward's Creek*, at the south end of the reach. The buildings at *Dunmore* stand three-fourths of a mile back, but are visible from the river. The cleared and cultivated fields to the southward of *Milton* and opposite to *Dunmore*, are part of the plantation of *Weynoak*, which occupies the whole width of the peninsula on this side. The creek that opens at the south end of the reach is *Ward's Creek*, and between this and *Weynoak Marshes* on the north side, the stream turns about west-northwest, so as to skirt the marshes, and then runs nearly due north again for nearly three miles.

On the west bank of the creek begin the bluffs, which extend beyond

Fort Powhatan.—This site is a high, bold, bare bluff, with an earthwork on top and a group of houses. It is directly opposite to *Weynoak Marshes*, and here the river is only one-fourth of a mile wide, deep from shore to shore, and has from fifty to ninety feet of water. The creek that makes in just above the fort is *Flower-dew Hundred Creek*, and forms the southern boundary of Flower-dew Hundred, a large plantation occupying the whole peninsula between this and the next reach.

As you pass *Fort Powhatan*, the view beyond is crossed **by** a very peculiar-looking red sand-bluff, appearing among the trees ahead, and a long stretch of yellow sand-bluffs continues to the westward until hidden behind *Windmill Point*. This is *Wilcox's*, and there is a wharf here directly opposite to *Windmill Point*, where we turn into the next reach. The wide creek on the north shore is *Court-house Creek*.

Windmill Point is low and thickly wooded. The river between it and Wilcox's turns nearly west, and we pass, first the plantations at *Flower-dew Hundred*, on the south bank, then the remarkable-looking *Westover House*, on the north bank, the former home of Gen. Harrison : and then about one and a half miles above Westover we see the ruins of a large wharf, and also a large dwelling and a few houses back. This is

HARRISON'S LANDING.

Harrison's Landing, famous in the late war as the place to which Gen. McClelland retreated after the seven days' fight in 1862. The wharf is on the plantation of *Berkeley*. The light-house seen ahead, but on the south bank of the river, is *Jordan's Point Light*, and the wide bay on the eastern side of it is *Tar Bay*. It is on the extremity of the point, and when you come abreast of it you see *City Point* ahead and about three miles off. Between *City Point* and *Jordan's Point* there is a deep bay formed on the south bank of the river, so that it is here one and three-fourths miles wide half way between the two points. City Point when first seen will appear of moderate height, pretty thickly settled, the houses interspersed with trees and cleared lands back, dotted here and there with scattered trees. The thickly-wooded point on the north bank just opposite is the south end of *Eppes' Island*.

City Point is the southern point of entrance to the *Appomattox River*. The *Appomattox*, on which were fought some of the bloodiest combats of the war, here opens to the westward, looking like a deep bay or bight owing to the wide opening at its mouth, suddenly contracting about a mile above to a width of about three hundred and fifty yards. This opening is nearly seven-eighths of a mile wide between *City Point* and *Bermuda Hundred*, the north point of entrance. This latter is high land, wooded in places, but mostly cleared and cultivated ; but where the settlement is, the land is low and covered with a scattered growth of trees. *City Point* was the great depot of supplies. etc., for the armies operating against Richmond in the war of 1861–65, and was for a time General Grant's headquarters. *Petersburg* is situated on the Appomattox south bank, a little over ten miles above its mouth.

At *City Point* the James turns abruptly to the northward, and runs in a nearly north-northeastly direction for three miles to the southeast end of *Turkey Island*. It gradually contracts its banks, being nearly three-fourths of a mile wide at *Bermuda Hundred*, and only about four hundred yards at the southeast point of *Turkey Island*. Here begins the great

Turkey Bend—the river skirting *Turkey Island*, in nearly a complete circle, being in no place more than one-half mile wide, and generally only about two hundred and fifty or three hundred yards wide. Turkey Island was the ancient seat of the Randolphs. Opposite *Bermuda Hundred* is the plantation of *Shirley* ; two and a half miles above *Shirley*, on the same bank, is *Haxall*—but there are no prominent features. All of this country was constantly being fought over during the war. On rounding Turkey Island and turning to the southward, the land on our right is *Curles' Neck*. The hills about a mile back, in a line with Turkey Island Creek, are

Malvern Hills, where was fought the bloodiest of the seven days' fight (1862). The creek opening to the westward as we come to this reach is *Curles' Swamp Creek*. The river rounds *Curles Neck* exactly as it does *Turkey Island*, and this bend is called *Curles' Bend*. The width between banks is from two hundred and fifty yards to three-eighths of a mile. The *Curles Plantation* is seen on the east bank, just as the river turns to the north.

Here is the *second bar* above *City Point*—the first one abreast of *Bermuda Hundred* with fourteen feet, and this opposite *Curles'* with thirteen feet. As a rule wherever the river widens above this you are crossing a shallow; the narrower the river the deeper it is. *Jones' Neck* is a long, narrow neck of land, edged with a dike, and the banks are mostly wooded. It begins opposite to *Curles'*, and extends to the northward a little over two miles, forming the banks on the left as we go up. A mile and three-eighths above *Curles'* is *Tilghman's Wharf;* and just beyond this the river turns again to the westward, rounding the north end of *Jones' Neck*, and then turning to the south along the west side of the neck.

Abreast of the north end of the Neck is *Four-mile Creek*, and on the western bank of this creek is

Deep Bottom, both famous in the history of the Army of the Potomac. Here was a *pontoon bridge*, where Grant crossed to the north bank of the James. The river is only about one hundred and seventy-five yards wide. From the north end of *Jones' Neck* it runs to the southward for one and one-half miles, and then nearly due west through a very pretty country for two miles to

Dutch Gap.—This famous place, so well known on account of the *canal* cut across it by General Butler's troops in 1864, is a very narrow neck of land, only about one hundred and fifty yards wide, which formerly joined *Farrar's Island* to the mainland, and the banks of the river, separated by this neck, are five miles above by the channel. The canal was not serviceable until after the Rebellion, and is only for small craft. A dike runs along its eastern and southern faces. In this bank was the *cave* in which the officer who controlled the torpedoes in the reach abreast of it had his apparatus.

At the *Dutch Gap Canal* the river turns about southsouthwest for a mile along the east shore of *Farrar's Island*, and then widening out turns due west for one and three-eighths miles, forming what is known as

Trent's Reach, contained between Farrar's Island on the north, and the mainland on the south. The reach at its widest part is six hundred yards wide. This was the scene of many combats during the summer of 1864. On the high banks on the south side was encamped the **Army of the James** at the time the famous "*bottling-u pro-cess*" went on; in the waters of the reach lay the fleet of gunboats and iron-clad monitors, and a line of torpedoes with wires leading to them from the batteries in the cave under the dike of Farrar's Island. The high bluff at the western end of the reach known as

Howlett's Bluff, was the Confederate battery known as Howlett's. Here on the 12th of June was fought the *battle of Howlett's Bluff.*

The river now rounds Farrar's Island, to the *west end* of *Dutch Gap Canal*, where it is only about one hundred and fifty yards wide. Now again it turns to the northwest to *Graveyard Reach*. The steep, prominent bluffs on the left above is the famous

Drewry's Bluff, the battery which so long defied the United States war vessels. It was however finally turned by Grant's army, and became of little importance. From this point to

Richmond is only fourteen miles, and the river is nearly straight, somewhat wider, and much shallower.

The *spires* of *Richmond* can be seen as soon as you pass the bend at *Drewry's*. Nearly seven-eighths of a mile above the northern end of *Richmond bar*, you will see what appears to be an island nearly in mid-river. This is *Drewry's Island*. The river passes on the east side of the island, and you will see the wharves, warehouses, and shipping at *Rochett's*, about three-fourths of a mile ahead on the east bank.

Rochett's is the southern *suburb of Richmond*. Here the river turns northwesterly, gradually widens, skirts the wharf-lines of *Richmond* and *Manchester*, and is crossed by bridges at the upper end of the reach. Here the channel-bed is filled with innumerable rocks and islands, through and among which run the dangerous rapids. *Manchester* is built upon the southwest bank, as *Richmond* is upon the northeast or right bank.

Richmond, in Henrico county, is beautifully situated. It was founded by Wm. Bird, in 1737, incorporated in 1742, and became the capital of Virginia in 1779-80. The capitol, built in 1796, is a fine structure, and, with other public buildings, stands on Shockoe Hill, a plain overlooking the river. The city has many ancient and excellent institutions of learning, beneficiary establishments, churches and monuments. The Washington monument presents one of the finest monumental groups on the continent. From 1861-65 Richmond was the capital of the Confederate States of America, and was evacuated (April 2, 1865,) upon the defeat of the Confederate forces and downfall of the Confederacy. The visitor will find much to interest him in and around the city.

EXCURSION V.

From Washington to Philadelphia, New York and Boston, by Sea.

DISTANCE FROM WASHINGTON

To SMITH'S POINT (Mouth Potomac) . .	119 Miles.	
To OLD POINT COMFORT	183	"
To PHILADELPHIA	431	"
To NEW YORK CITY	497	"
To BOSTON	789	"

TABLE OF DISTANCES

In *statute miles* from

OLD POINT COMFORT TO

	Miles.		Miles.
Capes Charles and Henry . . .	20	Sandy Hook Light Vessel . . .	288
Winter Quarter Shoal Light Vessel	101	Block Island	396
		Vineyard Sound (entrance) . .	431
Fenwick's Island Lighthouse .	141	Davis South Shoal Light Vessel	
Delaware Entrance	167	(outside course)	454
Cape May	173	Cape Cod L. H.	547
Five Fathom Bank Light Vessel.	166	Boston Entrance	597
Barnegat	238	Boston	606

Having reached OLD POINT COMFORT (FORTRESS MONROE) or NORFOLK by one of the commodious and elegantly appointed steamers from Washington—see EX-CURSION II. from Washington to the Mouth of the Potomac, and EXCURSION III., Mouth of the Potomac to Norfolk—the tourist or traveler will transfer to one of the large and staunch steamers of the ocean line, and may be prepared, with favorable weather, for a delightful and invigorating voyage.

Leaving NORFOLK, on passing *Hampton Roads*, bound for PHILADELPHIA, NEW YORK, or BOSTON, the steamer heads to abreast of the *red buoy* on the south-eastern end of the *Middle Ground*, twenty miles from Point Comfort. From this position, nearly in a line between *Cape Charles and Cape Henry*, it heads for the *whistling buoy* at the entrance to the Chesapeake Bay. Thence passes *Winter Quarter Shoal Lighthouse, Light*

(71)

Vessel, and *Hog Island Lighthouse.* When *Winter Quar-ter Shoal Light Vessel* is abeam, the course runs thirty-nine miles until *Fenwick's Island L. H.* bears west a distance of fourteen miles. At this point, if bound for

Philadelphia, the vessel steers for *Cape Henlopen,* at the entrance to the *Delaware Bay,* and thence up the bay and river. On this part of the voyage *Chincoteague Island L. H.* will be seen in the distance.

This island is famous for its breed of ponies, and the abundance and variety of its game and fish. There is also a popular summer resort on the island.

All the way from the capes of the Chesapeake to Boston will be seen numerous vessels, sail and steam, of all kinds and tonnage, coasters and foreign, carrying the commodities of different climes into our own seaports, or

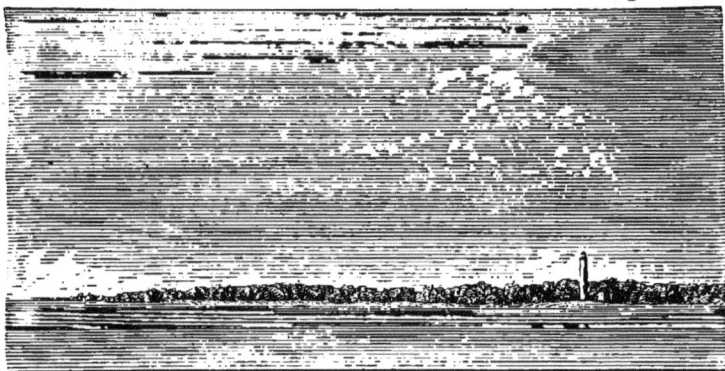

CAPE CHARLES (SEE P. 71).

outward bound, laden with the products of our own soil and industrial establishments. There will hardly be a moment in the day that the white wings of commerce will not greet the vision and enliven the vast watery expanse.

As the vessel approaches, *Cape Henlopen* will appear as a high ridge of bare white sand, surmounted by a tall lighthouse; and thence will enter the broad portals of the bay, with Cape Henlopen on the port and Cape May on the starboard side, and ascend to the metropolis of Pennsylvania, about ninety miles inland.

If the steamer be bound to

New York, when *Fenwick's Island* bears west, the course is to *Five Fathom Bank L. V.* From this point the course to *New York* runs eighty miles along the *New*

Jersey Coast, passing in view of *Absecom L. H.* nine miles, *Tucker's Beach L. H.* seven miles, and *Barnegat L. H.* seven miles off. The shore where seen appears simply as a dim blue line of woods. The immense fleets of vessels as far as the eye can reach will remind the voyager that the greatest seaport of the country is not far distant.

From *Barnegat L. H.* to *New York* the course will be forty-two miles to the *Sandy Hook L. V.*, and thence into *New York Bay.*

If bound to

Boston, the steamers usually pass outside of *Nantucket Shoals*, and therefore no land is seen from the time of leaving the entrance to the *Delaware Bay* until they make the eastern shore of *Cape Cod.*

CAPE HENRY (SEE P. 71).

Should the inner or *Vineyard Sound* course be taken from *Five Fathom Bank L. V.*, the steamer would head for *Block Island, Southeast L. H.*, and here steer for *Vineyard Sound*, and enter *Gay Head L. H.* on the east, and Vineyard Sound L. V. on the west, off the S. W. end of the Sow and Pigs Reef. On this course *Block Island* will be visible, and then the islands of the *Elizabeth Group.* The fleets of coasters take this track between New York and Boston.

By the usual course from the *Chesapeake* to *Boston*, outside of *Nantucket Shoals*, from off *Five Fathom Bank L. V.*, seldom visible, steamers steer for *Davis' South Shoals L. V.*, two hundred and eighty-eight miles. From this point they run for *Chatham Lights*, ninety-four miles, here making the first land since leaving the capes of the Delaware. Next to the northern one of these lights, at a distance of thirteen miles, will be seen the three *Nanset Beacons*, passed about four miles off, looking like three low towers on top of a white sand bluff. Next appear the spruce and fir-clad *Highlands of Cape Cod*, and surmounting them the *Cape Cod L. H.* Here the course changes to the westward to *Race Point L. H.*, on the eastern end of the cape, thence thirty-seven miles to BOSTON L. H. Between the *Cape Cod L. H.* and *Race Point L. H.*, the shore of *Cape Cod* is a mass of low sand hillocks, occasionally covered with grass, but mostly bare and undulating. The spires and houses of *Provincetown* are seen over the low sands. On the course for Boston, after leaving *Race Point*, is the famous MINOT'S LEDGE L. H. It appears as a lofty gray tower, one hundred feet high, apparently standing in the water, with the high, rocky shores near *Cohasset*, and a long, low sand spit, terminating in *Point Allerton*. The ledge upon which *Minot's* is built is only bare at low water. The construction of this lighthouse was a great engineering achievement. The larger houses on the shore are generally summer hotels.

After passing *Minot's Ledge L. H.*, will be seen a large *Bell Buoy*, which in heavy weather rings from the action of the sea, and warns mariners of *Harding's Ledge*. When past this, *Point Allerton* appears on the port, and when up to it, *Boston L. H.* on *Little Brewerton Island*. At this point BOSTON HARBOR is entered, and the voyage from Washington ended. The tall buildings of the city and prominent dome of the State House are visible from the steamer. The traveler after landing will have an ample field of sight-seeing at this historical and interesting city.

EXCURSION VI.

From Washington to Baltimore.

DISTANCE FROM WASHINGTON
    TO POINT LOOKOUT . . . . 106 Miles.
    TO BALTIMORE . . . . 190 "

TABLE OF DISTANCES TO POINTS

On the Chesapeake Bay, Compiled by the United States
Coast and Geodetic Survey.

FROM POINT LOOKOUT TO

	Miles.		Miles.
Point Look In	4	Holland's Point (Herring Bay).	45
Point No Point	7	Thomas Point	54
Cedar Point (Patuxent River)	17	Severn River (Annapolis)	58
Cove Point	19½	Highlands of the Magothy	63
Point of Rocks	23	Seven Foot Knoll Light	71
Sharp's Island	34	North Point	73
Plum Point	37	Baltimore	84
White Haven	42		

The tourist, taking a steamer at WASHINGTON FOR
BALTIMORE, will see EXCURSION II. for the voyage to
Point Lookout (mouth of the Potomac).

Point Lookout is the north point of entrance to the
Potomac, and one of the most important points on Chesapeake bay.

It is also the ter-
minus of the route of the *Washington and Point Lookout railroad.* This place will doubtless become a watering-place of importance.

Patuxent River is over four miles wide at its mouth at Cedar Point. It soon contracts, its banks being but half a mile apart at *Point Patience*, six miles above.

The *Patuxent River*, in 1813–14, was the scene of the gallant Commodore Barney's naval operations with his little flotilla of thirteen armed barges and schooner *Scorpion*, with an aggregate of five hundred men. Barney, threatened by an overwhelming force, in July, 1814, moved up the Patuxent to *Benedict*, and thence to Nottingham, to be able to co-operate against an attack on Washington or Baltimore. On August 16, the British squadron in the Chesapeake was reinforced by a fleet of twenty-one vessels, and having on board a strong land force. On August 18, five thousand British regulars and marines, and a number of impressed negroes, landed at Benedict, on the Patuxent. The British in the Patuxent moved up the river with their land force and a flotilla of barges. Reaching Nottingham, nineteen miles from Washington, with forty barges, August 22, they opened fire on the *flotilla*, which had taken refuge under Pig Point. Barney, with four hundred seamen, had joined

THE MOUTH OF THE PATUXENT.

Winder on the road to Washington, and Frazier, in obedience to instructions, when no longer able to hold his position against overwhelming odds, blew up his flotilla. The British land forces, under Ross, pressed on to Washington, and were joined in their march by Cockburn and his seamen and marines on August 23. Then followed the military movements which culminated August 24 in the stubborn conflict at Bladensburg, six miles from Washington, lasting from noon until 4 p. m., between about five thousand trained British troops and one thousand United States regulars, seamen, and marines, and four thousand raw militia, and ending in the flight of the bulk of the militia and the capture of Washington.

The bay at **Cove Point and Point of Rocks** is a little over five miles wide.

Sharpe's Island is one of the best known landmarks on the bay.

Between *Plum* and *Holland Points*, will be seen WHITEHAVEN and FAIRHAVEN, two favorite summer resorts. WYE *River*, opposite the latter, is the site of the ancient *Lloyd estate;* and here Edward Lloyd "of Wye" lived in patriarchal style, having, it is said, nine hundred slaves. A portion of his descendants still reside here.

The north side of the entrance to *Eastern Bay* is called *Kent Point*, and forms the southern extremity of **Kent Island**, famous for its fruit, especially peaches. Kent Island is over fourteen miles long, nearly level, and almost all highly cultivated.

In the estuary east of Kent Island, on the eastern shore of Maryland, at *St. Michael's*, Talbot county, is a village founded by ship-builders, and where most of the famous " Baltimore Clippers " of the War of 1812 were built. The British marauder, Cockburn, was determined to destroy the place, hearing that seven clippers were on the stocks. He accordingly made the attack in August. The ship-builders and the neighboring militia, at first surprised by the secrecy of the British movement, soon rallied. After a sharp conflict, the British, who outnumbered the Americans, were driven to their boats.

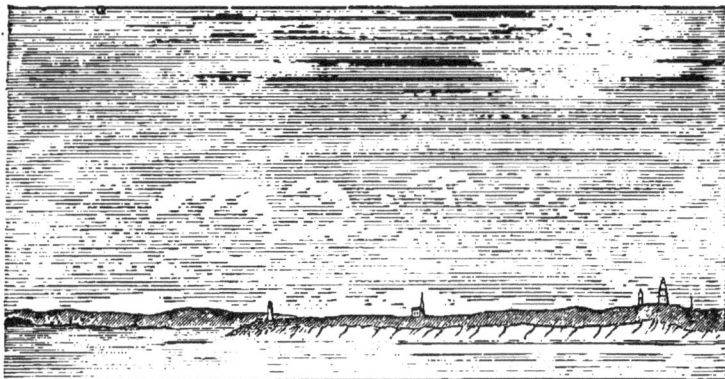

THE MOUTH OF THE SEVERN.

Above *Thomas' Point* is *Tally's Point*, the southern point of entrance to

Severn River, on which *Annapolis* is built. The shore here stretches in a long line of bare sand-bluffs, terminating at the point in a thickly-wooded bluff. The high dome seen over the land between this and *Thomas' Point* is the State House dome in Annapolis. The United States Naval Academy is also located here. The Severn is deep, but quite narrow.

Windmill Point, near Annapolis, was the scene of the grounding and burning of the ship Peggy, Captain Stewart, from London, having on board an assorted cargo, and seventeen packages—the first to arrive in the colony—of that proscribed article, tea. The people of Maryland took a decided stand against the tyrannous measures of the King and Parliament, beginning with the stamp act. The vessel arrived on Saturday, October 15, 1774. The following Wednesday a meeting of the people of the town and adjacent country was held at Annapolis. It was resolved to destroy the vessel and the tea; and under the advice of Charles Carroll, of Carrollton, later one of the signers of the Declaration of Independence, Anthony Stewart, the proprietor of the vessel, and who had paid duty on the tea for the consignees, set fire to her himself.

On the north side of *Sandy Point*, on the west shore of the bay, is the entrance to

Magothy River, and *"The Highlands of Magothy,"* a well-known landmark in coming up to Baltimore. The island on which the highlands are situated is known as *Gibson's Island.*

From this point to the mouth of the *Patapsco*, the scene is usually a very animated one, the waters being crowded with all kinds of craft. *Seven Foot Knoll L. H.,* is a little over one and a half miles off.

Bodkin Point the southern point and

North Point the northern point of entrance to the Patapsco.

HIGHLANDS OF THE MAGOTHY.

North Point was the scene of the landing of the British, September 12, 1814, comprising 5000 veteran troops, 2000 seamen, and 2000 marines, preliminary to an attack on Baltimore. The British fleet to co-operate on the river consisted of fifty sail. Ross, the British commander, boasted that he would dine in " Baltimore or hell " the following Sunday. In a desperate action the same day, seven miles from North Point, and the same from Baltimore, Ross was mortally wounded, and died before he reached the fleet. The Americans were finally overwhelmed, and withdrew to Fort McHenry. The enemy the next day moved up to the Fort, and made preparations for attack.

North Point is quite a summer resort. So also is *Shanon Point*, where is situated *Holly Grove.*

Abreast of Hawkins Point the river is only one and one-half mile wide ; and almost in the middle appear the remains of a granite fort standing in the water. This is

Fort Carroll, one side appearing to be broken down entirely. On its southern wall is a tower of open-work, which supports the light and fog-bell. *Fort Carroll* was built on the end of the shoal making off from *Soller's Point* on the north shore. There is a small settlement here.

THE MOUTH OF THE PATAPSCO (79).

BALTIMORE FROM THE HARBOR (79).

Leading Point is a bluff, sandy point, twenty feet high.
Fishing Point is two and a half miles below *Fort Mc-Henry.* Above *Fishing Point* makes in a wide arm of the river, which leads through *Smith's Cove* to *Ridgeley's Cove*, on the south front of *Baltimore.* On the north side of this entrance is

Fort McHenry, of famous memory for its successful defence, September 13–14, 1814, by a small garrison against a night assault supported by the whole strength of the British land and naval forces, flushed with the victory of *North Point.* It was the anxiety of the citizens of Baltimore concerning the fate of *Fort McHenry* that dreadful night, which suggested to Francis S. Key, of the Georgetown (D. C.) Light Artillery, the immortal lines of ``THE STAR SPANGLED BANNER.''

Fort McHenry appears when first seen as a large earthwork surrounding a fort of gray masonry, in the middle of which appear the barracks, painted yellow. The point on which the fort is built is graded to the slope of the glacis and carefully sodded.

Lazaretto Point, on the opposite bank, is known by the white light-tower on its extremity. At *Lazaretto Point*, the width of the river between it and Fort McHenry is but five hundred and fifty yards, but the depth is not less than twenty-six feet at low tide, and entirely unobstructed.

Passing between *Fort McHenry* and *Lazaretto Point*, we are in

Baltimore Harbor, and the city, with its wharves and shipping and buildings, is before and around us. The only noticeable natural feature is Federal Hill, with the remains of an earthwork on top, now utilized as the site of a pyramidal wooden structure, used as a signal tower for signaling the approach of vessels from the bay.

Vessels usually anchor off *Fell's Point*, which is directly ahead as the steamer approaches between *Fort McHenry* and *Lazaretto Point.* The cove to the eastward of it is called *Canton Hollow*, that to the westward is known as ``*The Basin.*'' This water is fresh, except in strong southerly winds; but it is not drinkable.

The tourist now leaves the steamer, and will find much to interest him in this beautiful metropolis.

www.ingramcontent.com/pod-product-compliance
Lightning Source LLC
Chambersburg PA
CBHW031453270326
41930CB00007B/975